museums and monuments XV

Titles in this series:

museums, imagination and education

unesco paris 1973

Published in 1973 by the United Nations
Educational, Scientific and Cultural Organization
7 Place de Fontenoy, 75700 Paris
Printed by Arts graphiques Coop Suisse

ISBN   92-3-101036-0
French edition: ISBN-92-3-201036-4
LC No. 72-97589

Preface

This publication is No. XV in the Unesco 'Museums and Monuments' series. The titles of previous issues in the series are listed elsewhere (they include No. IX, *The Organization of Museums: Practical Advice;* and No. X, *Temporary and Travelling Exhibitions*).

A number of issues of the Unesco quarterly *Museum* have been devoted wholly or in part to the educational role of museums.

Unesco sends experts and offers fellowships and equipment to help Member States in developing their museums. Seminars on the educational role of museums have been held in New York (1952), Athens (1954), Rio de Janeiro (1958), Tokyo (1960). (See article on 'Collaboration Between Museum and School'.)

At its eleventh session, on 14 December 1960, the Unesco General Conference adopted a Recommendation 'concerning the most effective means of rendering museums accessible to everyone'.

To the authors of the articles which make up this volume, Unesco would like to convey its very best thanks; the views expressed are those of the authors, and not necessarily those of the Organization.

Contents

Introduction

The thrill that students or children express on first seeing the exhibits in the galleries at a great museum never fails to impress me. It is a moment when eyes, hearts and minds, if not ears, are alert and receptive; when energies are stimulated and rearing to be unleashed. Even the most hardened secondary school boy or girl admits to interest being aroused at this moment, even if this is a mere flash in the gloom. Mere flash or more, it is a precious and vital moment.

This is how the second article in this collection begins. D. V. Proctor continues with a warning:

The energy and interest that are longing to be employed can so easily be dissipated, the emotion dulled, by a surly reception, by poor organization and frustrating delays, or even by hunger. . . . It is far more profitable to enjoy an hour or an hour and a half's concentrated viewing of a few galleries, than to attempt to visit a whole museum or a bewildering succession of museums and buildings.

Children would no doubt agree: with memories of aching feet (why is walking in a museum so much more tiring than walking elsewhere?), so would most adults.

The museum is radically changing, 'developing a social conscience, seeking to be of value and use to everyone' (W. S. Thomas). Some thirty years ago, in the United States, there were 50 million visits annually; the figure has grown to 300 million. The pattern is similar throughout the world.

Among the new visitors are many students and schoolchildren. Part of the change in the museum itself is due to an effort to cater for them. Louise Condit writes:

More progressive education in the thirties and forties, and the efforts of a handful of dedicated art educators gradually introduced a new philosophy, and new methods of teaching which aimed at allowing the child to nurture his originality and express his own ideas in a variety of materials. The emphasis was on doing; art appreciation as such was out of favour. With the increasing interest in all of the arts in recent years, however, and the rapid and widespread development of educational facilities and programmes in our art museums, there has been a renewed interest in enriching curricula by including art wherever it can be related to other subjects, in teaching the humanities—including some art history and appreciation—and even more specifically, in teaching children how to look at works of art. In many communities, these activities are being officially written into the curriculum from elementary level onwards.

This point is taken up from different angles. Renée Marcousé deals with the importance of learning to see and to think, rather than learning by heart:

In accordance with these prevailing ideas, less emphasis is placed on the formal concept of learning, in the museum, about objects as such. It is now assumed that children are not taken round galleries in large numbers, that they work individually or in small groups, that they do not merely listen to the expert but learn, by looking, how to distinguish differences in styles, in periods, and so on. A museum visit becomes an exciting venture; it has the element of personal discovery, of competition, which involves the child and puts him at ease. It is no longer a matter of listing names and dates, but of learning to recognize, visually, characteristics which differentiate centuries and countries, or the work of individual artists. This visual approach to learning is a special contribution of the museum, and applies to all age groups, at all stages of development.

How much can a child absorb? How much can a child resist? Can one take advantage of the wonders of a technological age and the facilities it offers and yet avoid superficiality? D. V. Proctor has full confidence in the child's discernment:

The child of 1970 is exposed to the dazzling effect of pressure salesmanship, of television and films; he is accustomed to watching presentations on the screen at home and in the local cinema, which have been prepared by teams of highly skilled men using sophisticated techniques, in order to capture and hold the attention of the onlooker. The same child is accustomed to the concept of rapid travel by car, ship, train and aeroplane, and to the reduction of the time and trouble it takes to travel across the world. Clocks, traffic-lights, barometers, speedometers and similar meters direct and control his daily routine. It is easy to think that these developments lure children away from the reality of objects, that their eyes and minds become quite blinkered. It is also easy to imagine that children have become restless and even more demanding than before.

But this is not so. The mind of the child is very quick to discern realities as opposed to fictions; to see beyond the celluloid world of the film or the television screen and to seek real things of beauty and value. Broadcast television programmes and films have spread knowledge and experience of great works of literature, of famous buildings, of facts of natural history, of science and of great art collections far wider and more quickly than has ever been possible before. . . .

In the article from Sweden on temporary and travelling exhibitions, we find the temporary exhibition, primarily educational in purpose, influencing the permanent in a novel way:

. . . It was shown at museums in Sweden for two years, and served to establish the 'activity room'

in exhibitions, since every museum receiving it had to set aside a space where teachers and pupils, parents and children and any other visitors could use various kinds of material—generally waste materials from local industries—for personal self-expression. In spite of the formidable practical difficulties at many museums, the activity room was a great success (not least with press photographers), and several schools have suggested that they be made a permanent feature of exhibitions.

The 'activity room' idea has caught on in many countries:

. . . Nothing has replaced and nothing will replace the impact of the real object, the experience of seeing, or better still of handling, the actual piece made by a great artist or used by someone many years ago. Expression of the thrill that this experience gives is seen in the wonderful and varied work produced by children and by students, in their willingness to come back and find out more or to go on elsewhere to discover further worlds of learning. Adults enjoy an enrichment of living and a broadening of horizons. So, like the great stained windows of a beautiful building, museums and galleries pour light of many colours and intensities in which we revel and grow, to our delight and to that of others [D. V. Proctor].

Sweden is a large country. Ulla Keding Olofsson points out that museums are responding to the demands created by more leisure and education by producing a wider range of exhibitions—which increase attendance figures but put a strain on resources (personnel, premises and money). She then quotes the *Belmont Report*, published by the American Association of Museums:

'The increase has been so rapid, and has reached such a level, that museums now have to turn down requests for service. Yet the times call for a sharp increase in the educational and cultural opportunities which museums are uniquely equipped to provide.

'The increased demands on museums come from all ages and segments of the population, affect not only the institutions in metropolitan centres but those elsewhere, and reflect the dependence on museums of both the disadvantaged and the affluent.

'So far as can be foreseen, the factors responsible for the increased demands on museums are likely to continue to prevail indefinitely.'

Sweden set up a government committee to investigate similar problems, and the article shows one of the ways in which they have been tackled, and the experiments 'with travelling exhibitions made in co-operation with museums, cultural agencies, education authorities, adult education services, government and regional bodies, and groups of artists'.

In a controversial book *Museums in the Seventies,* published in 1970, the heads of four Swedish museums argue that the increased attendance figures are illusory, that there are not new visitors but simply more visits by the same limited selection of people that have always visited museums. This is partly attributed to the nature of the exhibitions themselves—too little staff and money being available to make them attractive enough. The authors rightly stress the need for museums to extend their influence, socially and geographically; in this regard, the exhibition is simply one instrument among many.

The Soviet article is similarly concerned with reaching a distant public: the Moscow Polytechnic Museum also happens to be the headquarters of the society responsible for keeping the whole of the Soviet Union informed of the latest developments in science and technology.

Exhibitions dealing with modern science and technology are most in demand. Consequently, each section of the museum prepares a travelling exhibition on developments in its particular branch, in liaison with the industrial and research institutes that can provide information, instruments, samples, or finished products for exhibition purposes. The information is processed and sent in the form of an 'exhibition subject plan', together with diagrammatic and illustrative material, to the design studios for final production. Meanwhile, a brochure is compiled and published. A member of the section concerned travels with the exhibition to supervise its mounting and give any advice needed.

... With rare exceptions, only two men are needed for the loading, unloading and assembly, so that exhibitions can visit places which have no special handling equipment. For certain large-scale exhibitions (e.g. *Atoms for Peace* needing 400–500 square metres), special transport and equipment were needed. A full-time expert from the museum was assigned to this exhibition, and remained with it all the time it was on show.

The museum also arranges international exchanges of exhibitions under agreements for scientific and cultural co-operation.

Are there major differences as between developing and industrially advanced countries? Renée Marcousé considers it understandable that:

... in their present stage of development, museums of science and technology in developing countries should play a greater part in general education, and that the contribution of the art museum should appear less immediate. The former are not hampered to the same extent by earlier traditions; their exhibits for the most part relate to the present day; they provide a practical link with the past. Their contribution to education is especially noticeable in, for example, the work of the Birla Industrial and Technological Museum, Calcutta or in the Museum of Science, Cairo, where excellent demonstrations and special courses are organized in the museum as well as in the regional centres for the general public, for students and children of school age. In both instances, the student and teacher population are actively associated in this work and help in the preparation of the material. It is important, therefore, that new thinking in general education, with special reference to the aesthetic contribution of the art museum taking place in countries in the West, should be brought to the notice of developing countries.

The director of the Cairo Museum makes a number of original points on this same general subject. He, too, is a believer in the advantages offered by travelling exhibitions, and suggests some educational uses which would scarcely occur to those who still regard museums as a cross between a store-house and a mausoleum.

11

Developing countries have had their own civilizations. They have contributed much to man's knowledge. The young should know this bright history and accept the challenge to emulate it.

Nothing can help more than museums, which now are living institutions that can offer invaluable educational services to the new public. But museums need special buildings, a special design and much space. They cost a lot and need much effort and experience. If a developing country can afford to establish a museum it will usually be in the capital and thus confined to a limited public. The importance of travelling and temporary exhibitions becomes evident.

As the author also points out, children can go to schools and universities to prepare themselves for a future and better life, but many of the grown-ups have missed that opportunity. They are either completely illiterate or have very little education. As they are important parts of a living system working for economic development, educational services should be devoted to them.

Ancient and modern have a fascinating habit of proving less far apart in museums than the thousands of years that may separate them; and the ancient Egyptians could hardly have gone much further in condemning those responsible for pollution:

National history has its part. Drawings and writings from ancient Egyptian tombs show that no one could go to Paradise in the hereafter if he once polluted water. All Egyptians when about to die had to swear before the priest that they had never killed, never stolen and never polluted water. Again, a prescription for the treatment of bilharzia written over 4,000 years ago is shown, together with a modern prescription to show the near resemblance. The tomb in which bilharzia was first discovered, and the work of Ibn Sina, the Arab scientist who was the first to discover bilharzia and to write about it, also form part of the exhibit.

Finally, it is surely worth quoting another sentence from the article:

... The result of this experiment was the complete disappearance of bilharzia from the village.

India is another huge country. The richness and variety of its art is well known. Perhaps it is timely, accordingly, that the Indian contribution to this volume should deal with science museums and planetaria. These are important to the country's economic development.

One difficulty is mentioned which is not unique to India: a multiplicity of languages. Thus, at the Birla Planetarium, the largest in Asia, lectures have to be given in three languages: Bengali (the local language), Hindi and English; and occasionally in other languages.

But in India, it is difficult to isolate science from culture, and either from life generally:

In the circular gallery surrounding the dome, there are telescopic views of celestial bodies and star fields; busts of famous astronomers and thinkers; murals depicting the planets according to Hindu mythology (*Navagrahas*); and marble slabs with inscriptions from the *Vedas* and *Upanishads*. These have a particular charm for the Indian visitors, who listen with a religious zeal to talks on the vastness of space and the arrangement of the universe. . . .

And the stars and the gods link back to the market-place:

... A commercial firm was permitted to reproduce the *Navagrahas* (with due acknowledgement) in its calendars, one way of attracting religious-minded Indians to visit the planetarium. A coloured folder on the *Navagrahas* is to be published later. Postcards are available showing the projection instrument and views of the building, together with a brochure that discusses astronomy and gives details about the complex projection equipment.

The Curator of the National Museum of Niger does not rely on culture and education alone as arguments to refute the theory that museums are luxuries which developing countries cannot afford: he positively demolishes it by showing what has been done in the Niger.

When we first installed artisans in our open-air museum, the main purpose was ethnographical:

to preserve traditional techniques and let visitors
see them. But to be able to allow them to continue, we had to sell what they made. A gift
enabled us to set up a first stand. ... Consequently, we gave work to a large number of
craftsmen; this enhanced their standing; preserved traditional skills; gave new life to the
museum; made a modest contribution to economic development; and found additional funds
for the museum. ...

These results do not come automatically;
first:

Various deeply rooted prejudices had to be overcome. In many African countries, craftsmen have
always been looked down on. Even if the boys,
desperately needing to find some way to earn a
living, were quite happy to become craftsmen
(especially seeing how well off are those working
at the museum), the parents, or some of them,
were more than dubious.
It is silly and rather mad that men capable of
weaving, forging, carving or moulding such
splendid things should be looked down on by
people incapable of making anything with their
hands.

Again, the craftsmen must be:

... the best available, selected strictly on merit.
They must learn to respect agreed prices and
delivery dates. Objects must be examined one by
one, and anything badly made or ethnographically false rejected. A catalogue is necessary to
simplify foreign sales. Prices must be based on
real cost of production, so as to protect both
maker and buyer.

As for the actual museum, it would be difficult to find a more practical philosophy than
that displayed by the author and his colleagues:

The problem was to create a museum lively
enough to attract the people and be at the same
time educative. It had to interest the ordinary
people, those most in need of help. A museum
for the illiterate? Why not? At the risk of being
misunderstood, we decided to concentrate on
what we thought was most needed, to attempt a
compromise that would satisfy the educated without boring the illiterate. We believe we have

succeeded. At all costs, there must be nothing
sacred about the museum, and if the approval of
the educated visitor was precious, that of the uneducated was indispensable.

A wholly different aspect is dealt with by
John Read of the BBC:

Who sees these television programmes that feed
themselves on the possessions of the world's
museums? Millions of people, and certainly more
people than ever find their way into a museum.
We are active communicators in a mass medium.
We may debate how large a minimum-sized
audience can be, but there has never been any
debate about our need to communicate to our
audiences, large or small. If we fail, our audience
has gone and the programme might as well not
exist. In general, mass communication is a new
experience for museums and gallery staff. ...
    Where have we got to now? In the United
Kingdom, BBC Television produces and transmits 250 arts programmes every year. We endeavour, wherever the financial and legal possibilities exist, to sell as many of these as possible all
over the world. We join forces with other television organizations in order jointly to produce
and screen programmes that would not otherwise
be an economic proposition. We have even attempted to embrace all civilization in a single
series of thirteen 50-minute films written and
presented by Sir Kenneth Clark, a former Director of our National Gallery, and a world authority
who gave two years of his life to a project that
cost us £250,000 to make. Was *Civilization—A
Personal View* a museum without walls? Certainly museums all over the world contributed to
it, but what made the greatest impression were
those sequences filmed outside museums, in the
cathedrals, churches, cities, landscapes and buildings where the physical presence of great art in
its own setting gave the viewer an experience
rarely contrived in a gallery or a show-case.

So, through television, the museum has become international in a new sense.
    The author goes into some detail about the
problems of filming in museums. He fully
appreciates the inconveniences a film unit
may cause, but pleads for a more sympathetic
attitude on the part of some museum authorities—especially those who think there is
no limit to a television budget:

13

... I think people would welcome some agreed international scale of charges and a common procedure that would assure that a single payment allowed the television organization full rights to repeat its programmes and arrange their showing in other countries. As it is, we are approaching the stage when it would be cheaper to ask an artist to make a painting for us than to use a colour transparency of an existing work. Unfortunately there are not many people painting now called Rembrandt.

How do museums use the mass media? W. S. Thomas carried out a survey in the United States, receiving replies from 133 museums. His article neatly complements the Read article on a number of points. He finds, for example, that only 17 of the 133 museums replying now produce their own television programmes.

... Although the programmes were successful, most museums found that it cost too much to engage professionals; or that it took too much of staff time to plan programmes, select the material, and write the scripts; or that they had no witty expert available with the special personality needed in the master of ceremonies who puts its programme across.

However, both sides learned through working together on programmes:

As the professional scientist learned the values of showmanship, the professional broadcaster gained an increasing respect for scholarship. Methods were developed to set the dramatic highlight against the background of solid information, to check extreme erudition with popular appeal, and to maintain accuracy in spite of simplification and focus. The result was highly effective museum television.

Apart from, as well as in conjunction with television, what was the attitude to film? The article states that:

Museums have never gone in for film production as widely as they might, despite their wealth of prospective subjects and staff expertise, chiefly because of the cost and the necessity of securing professional aid: 27 per cent had films made for them by commercial firms; only 10 per cent used the film institutes or audio-visual departments of universities and foundations; 4 per cent had their films made by volunteers.

Despite the more spectacular qualities of television:

... radio has specific advantages for museums as an educational and information medium. Radio programmes are cheaper to produce, need less staff and do not as a rule involve the handling of valuable museum objects; if they have news value they may be more easily used and hence, more freely accepted. And programme time is contributed free by most local stations.

But, from the point of view from which the article is written, the daily newspaper:

... remains perhaps the museum's most reliable outlet for information and popular education. There were 1,752 daily newspapers in the English language in the United States in 1969, with a combined circulation of 62,535,394; and all museums, no matter how small, have news which can be used in the local press.

Radio and television may reach more people, but the local newspaper is a steady and reliable user of a wide range of local news, and even if only one person in each family reads the papers, information spreads rapidly by word of mouth.

Renée Marcousé points out that emphasis on direct involvement, on personal discovery, on creative activity—music, dance, drama, as well as related interests (archaeology, history, geology)—is characteristic of a new approach to education which is now encouraged in the museum as in the school and should be of special interest to countries where the visual cultural tradition has not been replaced by a wholly conceptual approach to learning.

She quotes the example of Indonesia, where:

... education still relates to the culture and art interest of the people. One might indeed say that here, there is tangible evidence of education through art, for it is by means of an instinctive need and pleasure in dance, drama and music that education is encouraged and fostered, and there is as yet little evidence of children or adults learning by heart in the museum in a manner derived from the West. . . .

Thailand, another developing country with a great visual tradition, presents an interesting contrast to Indonesia:

. . . Western influence has here accentuated the conceptual rather than the visual and creative approach in education; this is in part due to the intensive modernization and development of the country's economy during the past decade, and the priority given to science and technology. . . .

She describes a number of experiments which differ considerably in scope and approach, and recalls that:

. . . In each case, it is the imaginative understanding of individual circumstances and needs which brought these centres and museums into being. Each relates to a particular background, and their success is due in large measure to the involvement of their public. In these areas, the collections have become identified as their collections. This is a new point of departure for the teacher and curator, and opens up new possibilities of education through museums.

Louise Condit also quotes some fascinating examples, including the pioneering *Children's Art Carnival*. She describes the wealth of creative art classes that are now run in conjunction with museum programmes:

. . . drawing, painting, sculpture, ceramics, mosaics, mask-making, collage and assemblage, puppetry, print-making, batik, weaving, rug-making, photography, film-making, kite-making, liquid graphics, dance, drama, poetry, jazz—all can be found in American museums. As a rule each class is offered for a specific, rather narrow age range, sometimes beginning as low as age 3. However, a number of museums offer classes for children and parents together; these are a popular and effective way of involving parents in today's art education.

There is a trend in primary and elementary education in the United States:

. . . towards providing freer, less-structured educational environments, and placing more emphasis on learning than on teaching. A wealth of carefully selected materials is provided, and children are invited to discover for themselves what the materials can do. The underlying purpose is to preserve the joy of learning which very young children exhibit so conspicuously and, at the same time, to obtain first-hand practical experiences to provide a firm foundation for future thinking.

[But museums] . . . hardly ever have formal, official relationships with schools, covering educational policy, standards, budget, and division of responsibility. Instead, on their own initiative, they have developed programmes and found funds to support them, and then offered them free or at a nominal fee to children and to schools . . .

How far should museums have more official relationships with schools?

Speaking from Polish experience, André Szpakowski indicates how co-operation could be much more effectively arranged than it is today (the word museum being taken in a very wide sense). The museum authority would need to have a fairly detailed knowledge of the school programme, and choose themes which could be so treated in the museum as to complement the curriculum. This does not mean going to the other extreme, when the teacher expects the museum to be a kind of annex to illustrate the subjects he teaches.

There are obvious difficulties; finding the time for visits, finding the staff to cope with the extra work involved in both school and museum, and so on. The author believes firmly enough in the educational potentiality of the museum to consider it worth while to overcome them.

The last article is described as 'an annotated bibliography of the growth of an idea'. The idea does not date from yesterday . . .

There have been many noble and creative ideas regarding the use of museums for the public good, some dating from as long ago as in the ancient museum, library and research centre at

Alexandria. Some have remained plans and dreams only, like Mundaneum, conceived by Paul Otelet and designed by Le Corbusier in the 1930s for the League of Nations. It was to be a universal museum and library centre, in the form of a ziggurat; the visitor would be taken to the top of known history by elevator and then, by means of a circular ramp, walk back down through displays of culture through the ages. It was never built but the idea probably influenced Frank Lloyd Wright in designing the Guggenheim Museum.

The author suggests that:

... Reproductions of paintings and sculpture, photography, programmed slides, programmed films, recordings of music and speech, cultural history should show the unbroken line from the earliest times to our own, with materials so ordered that both the chronological sequence of a particular culture and a cross-section of a culture at a particular time could be examined. Far from being a sterile mausoleum containing a few originals, the museum should provide a bridge from instruction to enlightenment.

From the article 'Children and Art', one more point is worth emphasizing:

... teachers are frequently amazed to observe how well slow learners and poor readers respond when the questions can be answered by looking at real objects; and museum lecturers are often astonished to learn that an especially responsive class whose members have made acute and original observations, is 'the slowest in the school'. . . .

There is surely a lesson here for all educators.

Reading through these articles with a view to preparing an introduction, one quality emerges as being common to the articles themselves, to the various solutions countries have found, to the contents of museums, to the quality of art itself, to the very idea of enlisting museums to further education in the broadest sense. That quality is imagination. It seemed right to introduce it into the original working title for this book.

Renée Marcousé

Changing museums in a changing world

1

Education in museums is becoming a key word in countries in all parts of the world. Museums as such have taken on a new significance; they have become more closely identified with their national heritage, with cultural status. Above all, in the new social conditions of today, they are no longer looked on as the prerogative of an élite but are expected to be accessible, understood, appreciated and enjoyed by all. This new attitude is one of two significant changes; the second relates to the public who now frequent them in ever-increasing numbers. This public, called 'new' to emphasize the change in outlook and background, is of today; it is, in effect, the product of the political, economic and social developments of the past twenty-five years. It is found in the East as in the West, in developed as in the developing countries, and this factor must be taken into account in any assessment of international trends in museums today. The needs and demands of this public have played a decisive part in the general policy to publicize, popularize and integrate museums more fully into everyday life by means of the educational and cultural activities which are changing the museum image from that of a quiet backwater to a hive of activity. These changes, to some extent, cut across boundaries imposed by background and tradition, but the latter have still to be taken into account in any assessment of education in museums.

Renée Marcousé was formerly Director of Education Services, Victoria and Albert Museum, London.

In developing countries there are those who are evolving museum techniques directly related to present-day conditions and social needs, and those who, despite independence, limit their functions to those of an earlier period. Art museums in India, for example, are for the most part concerned with prestige, scholarship and research; this in itself is highly commendable, provided the requirements of an increasingly museum-minded public are not overlooked. It is no easy matter to adjust these priorities, and even in the United Kingdom and other Western countries, education is only now being accepted as an integral part of the museum's responsibilities to its public.

It is understandable that, in their present stage of development, museums of science and technology in developing countries should play a greater part in general education, and that the contribution of the art museum should appear less immediate. The former are not hampered to the same extent by earlier traditions; their exhibits for the most part relate to the present day; they provide a practical link with the past. Their contribution to education is especially noticeable in, for example, the work of the Birla Industrial and Technological Museum, Calcutta, or in the Museum of Science, Cairo, where excellent demonstrations and special courses are organized in the museum as well as in the regional centres for the general public, for students and children of school age. In both instances, the student and teacher population are actively associated in this work and help in the preparation of the material. It is important, therefore, that new thinking in general education, with special reference to the aesthetic contribution of the art museum taking place in countries in the West, should be brought to the notice of developing countries.

In accordance with these prevailing ideas, less emphasis is placed on the formal concept of learning, in the museum, about objects as such. It is now assumed that children are not taken round galleries in large numbers, that they work individually or in small groups, that they do not merely listen to the expert but learn, by looking, how to distinguish differences in styles, in periods, and so on. A museum visit becomes an exciting venture; it has the element of personal discovery, of competition, which involves the child and puts him at ease. It is no longer a matter of listing names and dates, but of learning to recognize, visually, characteristics which differentiate centuries and countries, or the work of individual artists. This visual approach to learning is a special contribution of the museum, and applies to all age groups, at all stages of development.

This emphasis on direct involvement, on personal discovery, on creative activity— music, dance, drama, as well as related interests (archaeology, history, geology)—is characteristic of the open-ended approach to education which is now encouraged in the museum as in the school. These methods relate to the prevailing background in each country; they are not yet common practice in the United Kingdom or in other Western countries, but they are indicative of changes in education as such, and should be of special interest to countries where the visual cultural tradition has not been replaced by a wholly conceptual approach to learning.

In Indonesia, for example, education still relates to the culture and art interest of the people. One might indeed say that here, there is tangible evidence of education through art, for it is by means of an instinctive need and pleasure in dance, drama and music that edu-cation is encouraged and fostered, and there is as yet little evidence of children or adults learning by heart in the museum in a manner derived from the West. Faced with problems of economic development and of education, it is therefore timely to point the increasing significance now attached to the place of the arts and crafts by advanced countries and through societies such as the International Society for Education through Art (INSA). Their experience and the pilot studies in art and education instigated by bodies such as the Schools Council in the United Kingdom could be of practical value in co-ordinating formal conceptual learning with art. It would indeed be lamentable if the experience of the advanced countries which are now trying to remedy the neglect of the arts and crafts in their educational system was not made known to countries who face similar problems, although in different circumstances and at a different period of time.

Thailand, another developing country with a great visual tradition, presents an interesting contrast to Indonesia. Western influence has here accentuated the conceptual rather than the visual and creative approach in education; this is in part due to the intensive modernization and development of the country's economy during the past decade, and the priority given to science and technology. It is, however, to be hoped that their long-standing skills in art and crafts will also be used to effect, and that the increasing importance given to them in education in advanced countries will, in schools and museums, stimulate new creative activities and visual learning.

The situation elsewhere, in Africa, Latin America and the Islamic countries differs in detail, but there is a common problem—how to educate large numbers of adults and children, how to associate modern techniques and methods with existing traditions so that, regardless of the subject or the learning situation, each becomes interested in the actual process of learning. The open-ended approach to museum education, with its insistence on visual as well as conceptual teaching, has much to offer. It does not follow, however, that the same solutions apply everywhere, or that methods successful with a particular group may not fail lamentably in another setting. It is a matter of enlightened adaptation in methods of work to meet the needs and conditions of each situation rather than blind imitation of one concept or of one approach to teaching.

Certain developments taking place today in the form of children's clubs and adult centres are another facet of museum education. These centres are set up either by museums or by organizations working in close association with them. They are, as it were, an extension of the museum proper, designed to meet the needs of a particular group or interest and, in general, provide facilities for individual and creative work. This active participation by members is part of a new relationship with the museum itself. Of special interest in this respect are the Neighborhood Museums (United States), children's centres as at the Bal Bhavan (New Delhi) and Muse (Brooklyn, New York).

The Neighborhood Museum, a relatively recent development in the United States, is becoming increasingly popular throughout that country. It has something in common with the community centres elsewhere, but relates more directly to the museum. Its aim is not only to bring the museum to people who, for economic and social reasons, rarely leave their neighbourhood, but also to identify them closely in its preparations, displays and activities. The exhibits often relate to the particular district. The following extract is taken from Dillon Rippley's account of the Neighborhood Museum at Anacosta, Washington, D.C., started by the Smithsonian Institution:

An unoccupied theatre was rented, the seats removed and a flat floor installed. The exhibits resulted from a number of suggestions, primarily from the advisory council but also from the Smithsonian staff curators. A complete general store just as it existed in Anacosta in 1890 occu-

pies one corner. In it is a post office which we hope to get licence to operate, old metal toys, a butter churn, an ice-cream maker, a coffee grinder and a water pump, all of which can work, and any number of objects of the period from kerosene lamps, flat irons, to posters and advertisements. There is another do-it-yourself area for plastic art with, at present, volunteer class-instruction. There are skeletons of various kinds, some of which can be put together ... some disassembled. There is space for temporary art shows, there is a television monitor system on the stage. Occupying one of the modules is a living zoo with monkeys, a parrot, and a miscellany of animals on loan from the National Zoological Park. A great success was a shoe-box museum— an A-frame structure full of wooden shoe-boxes containing bird skins, mammal skins, shells, fossil specimens, pictures and slide projectors for extensive handling and study. A behind-the-scenes museum exhibit of leaf making, silk-screen techniques, casting and modelling, gives an additional outlet for instruction. This has incited some members to go further afield and visit other museums.[1]

Muse, a centre for 'teens and adults' is run by the Brooklyn Museum, New York. This has been specially cited on account of its innovation programmes for children and the development of neighbourhood participation. It runs a variety of workshops where members receive instruction and can pursue their own interests. These include: Having Fun with Words (ages 6–8); Writer's Workshop (ages 9–12); Anthropology Workshop (ages 10–14); Photography Workshop (age 17 and upwards); Dance Workshop (age 15 and upwards); Aviation Workshop (age 15 and upwards). There is a loan service and certain items can be borrowed; this is an inspired way to involve members and open the door to further activities of all kinds.

These are museums of a new kind, and as specialist in their way as some of the older institutions. The object remains the central point, but one emphasizes the more traditional functions of conservation and presen-

1. Dillon Rippley, *The Sacred Grove*, New York, N.Y., Simon & Schuster, 1969.

tation, where as the other is more concerned with the imaginative role of the object in relation to its public. In the latter case the public itself, school child and adult, have been involved in the preparation of the collection. In each case, personal involvement led to a fuller understanding of the object, as well as a new awareness of the more conventional aspects of the museum's functions.

The Bal Bhavan in New Delhi is a children's centre; its setting and background provide an interesting comparison with Muse, and demonstrates the difficulties of adapting ideas successful in one country for use in another. It is so popular that, in order to allow the maximum number the use of the workshops, members have to be strictly limited to a few hours' attendance per week. Situated in spacious grounds, it has well-equipped workshops for pottery, painting, music, dance and drama; there is also a children's museum which is open to members but is used more by visiting school parties. From an educational point of view, this venture is forward-looking and relates to the new learning situations being tried out in the West, where children are encouraged to create, to work and to think as individuals.

In the more affluent West this idea is acceptable and encouraged, but in India it is a new departure, and many parents consider time spent in this way to be wasteful when the children might otherwise be at work, helping the family. Basic education is accepted, but creative activities and the rest are in the nature of frills and, as such, are unacceptable. Parental opposition to new ideas in education is by no means unknown in any country, and indeed the open-ended teaching methods being tried out in the United Kingdom are still viewed with suspicion by many adults. In the Bal Bhavan, however, the difficulty is practical, economic pressure. It is no easy task in these circumstances to encourage creativity and help the child to develop as an individual while still maintaining his sense of responsibility towards the family. Yet, ultimately, this will lead to the effective growth

and acceptance of these new ideas by a new generation.

This attitude is in striking contrast to the underlying ideas of the art centre planned in Bali for secondary school children which is to be devoted to painting, dance and music. In each instance, however, the traditional cultural background has to be taken into account, and for the Balinese, music and dance have economic as well as educational value.

The new role of the public and its active participation in museum matters is further illustrated in two examples from the United Kingdom—the Avoncroft Museum of Buildings, Bromsgrove, and the Ripley St Thomas School Collection of Agriculture and Rural Life.

The Avoncroft Museum of Buildings was started through the efforts of a residential teacher-training college and a group of inspired amateurs who collaborated to save a fifteenth-century merchant's house from demolition. From this initial effort the museum emerged as a charitable trust and limited company by guarantee. Its immediate concern is to stimulate public interest in the conservation of the smaller buildings with which the National Trust cannot cope. Valuable relations have developed with the local teacher-training college and with primary and secondary schools. Teachers, lecturers and children are involved in the work of the museum. For example, a local classics master has erected an Iron-Age hut and will dig trenches to experiment with the storage of grain. Two young engineers volunteered to demolish a decayed timber windmill for reconstruction on the museum site; the brickwork base was handled by boys from the local Borstal institution who, with guidance, will reconstruct the round house. The museum's carpenter, helped at times by his huge family, has worked on the site since the beginning, and will start a school of carpentry for the restoration of timber buildings. Students from the local teacher-training college take children to study and create in this sturdy, open-ended situation, where things are actually happening. This is indeed an example of total co-operation between the museum and the public, and this public includes children as well as adults.

At Ripley St Thomas the collection, begun to meet a school's specific need, was made possible by the active participation of the pupils. One of the masters says:

The idea arose from discussion on the speed of change taking place in methods of farming; it was suggested that we might collect some of the items which were passing out of use. Premises were available, the school having taken over a small adjoining farm as a rural science unit. When we announced that we were starting a collection of farm implements, the word spread quickly through the area and many children informed us of things they had seen lying derelict in fields or barns. As each item is collected we try to restore it to something like its original state. This process is fairly simple with small items, but a reaper which has been lying in the open for ten years took some six months to restore to a working state. The children who undertake this work learn about machinery and begin to understand about a particular branch of farm work. We hope to set up a farm kitchen so that they may see how the farmer lived in the age before mechanization.

Muse, the Bal Bhavan, Anacosta, the Avon-croft Museum of Buildings and the collections at Ripley St Thomas are singled out from amongst many other developments because of their special relevance outside their own neighbourhood and country. In each case, it is the imaginative understanding of individual circumstances and needs which brought these centres and museums into being. Each relates to a particular background, and their success is due in large measure to the involvement of their public. In these areas, the collections have become identified as their collections. This is a new point of departure for the teacher and curator, and opens up new possibilities of education through museums.

The museum's closer contact with the public of today underlines the need for fuller information about these visitors—their background, their preferences, their reactions to methods and techniques now in use; such knowledge is vital to the success of further work and developments. Audience surveys are being made in India, the Netherlands, Poland and the U.S.S.R.; the results will appear in shortened form in the *ICOM Annual,* and the complete report will be published in English and Russian by courtesy of the U.S.S.R. National Committee for ICOM.

In view of many new developments in museum education, it is natural that increasing attention is being given to the training required for the educationalist in the museum, and for the teacher who integrates the museum visit with the school curriculum. General courses in museology now offered by universities in many parts of the world are primarily concerned with matters of conservation, presentation and research. A Working Party on Training set up by the ICOM Committee for Education and Cultural Action has drawn up recommendations concerning the general qualifications and status of the museum educationalist, and proposes that these recommendations be put into effect in the current courses on museology and that the training of the educationalist be given full consideration in their programmes of study.

These are some of the international trends that can be distinguished in museum education. It is neither possible nor desirable to work out detailed adaptations and variations for different countries. It is the general picture of change, with its growing emphasis on different forms of participation by the public, which is of special interest; to understand how the museum is adapting its traditional functions to open-plan education within and without its walls, so that it becomes more fully integrated into the everyday life of both child and adult.

D. V. Proctor

Museums—teachers, students, children

2

The thrill that students or children express on first seeing the exhibits in the galleries at a great museum never fails to impress me. It is a moment when eyes, hearts and minds, if not ears, are alert and receptive; when energies are stimulated and rearing to be unleashed. Even the most hardened secondary school boy or girl admits to interest being aroused at this moment, even if this is a mere flash in the gloom. Mere flash or more, it is a precious and vital moment. The energy and interest that are longing to be employed can so easily be dissipated, the emotion dulled, by a surly reception, by poor organization and frustrating delays, or even by hunger. I recall one boy of about 10, who had only been given a banana for breakfast and who had subsequently made a 200-mile journey to reach the museum. He was so hungry and so emotionally overwhelmed on entering it that he fainted and had to retire to the local hospital for treatment. I am afraid he saw very little of the collections that day. Thus, even the most commonplace factors have to be remembered when organizing a visit. For on the one hand there is the museum, a storehouse of great treasures and, on the other, a group of young people eager to enjoy and learn from them. The important and enjoyable responsibility for seeing that energies are properly directed and emotional responses well served is shared jointly by the teacher or leader of the group and by the museum staff. This requires skill, experience and knowledge on both sides.

Museums and galleries offer the visitor a scintillating array of the treasures of man's past. Treasures in various forms, ranging through man's highest artistic achievements, his scientific discoveries, his progress in technology, his means of travel, exploration and discovery, his everyday life, his struggles with his own kind and natural background. Such treasures and supporting documentary material are conserved and displayed in the great national collections found in important cities and in the lesser, but for some equally desirable, provincial museums, chateaux, castles, country houses and folk museums. All combine to offer people a display of life at its various levels and backgrounds through different periods of history. From Stonehenge to the Taj Mahal the student or child may discover for himself the pleasure of learning more about the past and hence, about himself.

For the student, whether at college or of more adult age, libraries, reading rooms, catalogues and indexes of information are made available, so that he can pursue a particular line of study in depth and in convenient and tranquil surroundings. Usually the scholarship of the curator is available for students through museum publications on sale at the bookstall, through journals in the reading room or through personal discussion. To avoid wasting time and energy, these discussions have usually to be arranged in advance, and are most successful when the

D. V. Proctor is Education Officer at the National Maritime Museum, Greenwich, United Kingdom.

student has material carefully prepared. They form a most valuable and important contact between the informed adult and the staff of a museum, providing a chance for mutual encouragement and exchanges of knowledge.

The child of 1970 is exposed to the dazzling effect of pressure salesmanship, of television and films; he is accustomed to watching presentations on the screen at home and in the local cinema, which have been prepared by teams of highly skilled men using sophisticated techniques, in order to capture and hold the attention of the onlooker. The same child is accustomed to the concept of rapid travel by car, ship, train and aeroplane, and to the reduction of the time and trouble it takes to travel across the world. Clocks, traffic-lights, barometers, speedometers and similar meters direct and control his daily routine. It is easy to think that these developments lure children away from the reality of objects, that their eyes and minds become quite blinkered. It is also easy to imagine that children have become restless and even more demanding than before.

But this is not so. The mind of the child is very quick to discern realities as opposed to fictions; to see beyond the celluloid world of the film or the television screen and to seek real things of beauty and value. Broadcast television programmes and films have spread knowledge and experience of great works of literature, of famous buildings, of facts of natural history, of science and of great art collections far wider and more quickly than has ever been possible before. Specially prepared educational programmes have supported this informal dissemination of knowledge and experience with more formal teaching. Much depends on home background and the encouragement given by parents, but in general, far from leading children away from real objects of beauty or from real experience of science and natural history, these media have acted as introductory communicators and have led children to seek the real things, to go and see for themselves. Improved transport facilities have

meant that the business of travel is easier and cheaper. Thus today's child has much more preparation, and his critical faculties are far more developed than yesterday's child, and he is stimulated to see the real thing for himself.

An increased emphasis on the organized educational use of art-gallery and museum collections has occurred simultaneously with the developments noted above. To no small extent the impetus for this has come from within the museum profession and the teaching profession. The phase of struggle to re-establish and to re-vitalize existing museum educational services in the post war years is over. Expansion on the old foundations has taken place, and many new services have been formed, bringing an influx of fresh minds and energy, demanding higher standards and more effective approaches.

The wave of increased interest from children and students has given further stimulation. Now it is not at all unusual to find that, in place of one officer, several education staff have been appointed, that in place of a dingy remote corner of the museum which no one else wanted, they have been given well-fitted teaching rooms, club rooms and studios in which to work. Although some curators still fear the spread of museum educational services, many have recognized their value in making soundly organized provision for visitors, thus easing the load of work on the purely curatorial staff, giving them more chance to carry out their research and writing. Good standards in educational work are achieved only through hard work and the appointment of well-qualified staff, so that the education department of a museum can stand on a par with the curatorial departments in efficiency and in general academic ability.

Recently there has also been a revolution in teaching methods in schools. Old, formal methods, relying almost entirely on the teacher as the supreme authority and the written and spoken word as the method, have given way to more liberal and flexible methods in which the teacher shares whilst he supervises learning with the children. The teacher encourages his children to find things out for themselves. In addition to classroom libraries the school provides collections of objects for the children to handle and thus to gain experience and knowledge. Filmstrips, slides, tape recordings, films and closed-circuit television introduce the children to learning from collections and buildings outside the classroom. But the good teacher does not rely on these classroom visual and oral experiences alone. He actually takes the class out to see the real things and shows the children how to learn from them. Class visits to museums and galleries are a regular part of any good teacher's methods.

A revolution has also occurred in the syllabus and in the aims of teaching. Although not as widespread as the change in methods, a firm movement away from a cramping syllabus of work aimed almost solely at achieving good examination results has begun. Instead of filling a child's mind with facts and teaching it to retain and disgorge these in an order suitable for answering an examination question, the teacher trains the child to observe, question and analyse, and to be prepared to marshal and reproduce his knowledge in such a way that he can show powers of appreciation, self-expression, judgement and application. A learning project is set in which the interrelationship of several subjects—art, language, mathematics, geography—is taught, leading to the acquisition of knowledge in depth on the theme of the project. Thus a project on a voyage of exploration will lead to the study of the ships and their construction; of navigation and hence mathematics; of geography; of the social customs of the voyagers and the peoples they meet; of the language of these groups; of meteorology and of commercial and political history. Art teaching will lead to practice in the illustrative representation of the subjects and by encouraging the children to imagine they are taking part in the voyage the skilful teacher can lead them to express their adventures and emotions in the

spoken and written work of their own language. Important stimulation to write and to acquire more knowledge is gained from seeing the contemporary objects illustrating these subjects displayed in a museum or gallery where in addition, their historical context is also explained.

Realizing the importance of this moment when so much interest is being shown in collections and so much use being made of them, the museum profession has not only encouraged the development of individual museum education services, but has provided forums for the discussion of methods and aims and for the examination of standards. National groups such as that in the Netherlands and the Group for Educational Services in Museums in Britain hold conferences, run courses and provide advisory services. These national groups have received official recognition and encouragement from government departments. Through the generous assistance of the Soviet Government, the International Council of Museums (ICOM) organized a special meeting of its International Education Committee in Leningrad and Moscow in 1968. This meeting reaffirmed the value of forming national groups and suggested the following subjects for study to stimulate a two-way flow of ideas between those using museums and those working in them: Museum and School; Museum as a Cultural Centre; Problems of Perception; and Technical Aids.

As these national and international initiatives have re-emphasized, the educational use of a museum is no longer a matter for a casual approach. The proper use of a museum collection requires special skills on the part of both the museum and the teaching staff. The excursion visit 'to see what is in such and such a museum' on a wet afternoon in place of sports, or as part of a vaguely defined educational tour, is recognized for the disaster it is. Disaster because it gives neither the visitors nor the museum a fair and proper chance. The all too common habit of cramming as much sight-seeing as possible into an 'educational excursion', in the belief that this is the way to obtain maximum benefit is also recognized as a myth. A successful visit to a museum or art gallery is the result of careful preparation, otherwise a child may be put off visiting museums for good or at least bored stiff and completely muddled. In illustration of this I well remember the occasion when a group of schoolchildren came to the National Maritime Museum having, like so many other groups, already crammed in a visit to Westminster Abbey with guided tour, to the Houses of Parliament, to the Tower of London and a boat trip (with commentary) down the river Thames. With limp limbs and minds reduced almost to porridge, they staggered into the museum quite unfit for any further visiting.

The new syllabus and methods of teaching, the fresh approach to museums all demand much of the teacher. Many, but not all teacher-training colleges devote some time to the training of students in the techniques of using museums and to the appreciation of their educational vitality. This is an important contribution and introduces the concepts of museum education at a good moment, when the young teacher has a chance to digest the subject, which he will probably not have much time to do at a later stage in his teaching career. Many museums and galleries play an active part in these courses for students, arranging discussion and lecture sessions at the museum and encouraging students to bring parties of children. In some cases students are allowed to teach in the galleries as part of their practical training. Many museums also offer short courses for teachers, sometimes in co-operation with an in-service teachers' centre. These courses are organized in conjunction with education authorities, so that they are presented at times and in a manner best calculated to help the practising teacher. This form of liaison in the training of teachers produces extremely valuable results because it gives them a real insight into the value of a museum or gallery.

When preparing a visit the teacher or leader of a group of students should make a reconnaissance visit to the museum, to determine for himself the nature of the collections and, if possible, to make advance arrangements with the education staff. Where this is not possible, the teacher can at least write or telephone to give the museum warning of his intended visit and to ask for advice. This is far better than infuriating the curators and frustrating the children or students by arriving at a maritime museum expecting to find a display on the history of farm implements; such things do happen. In any case, good manners demand that the museum be informed of the proposed arrival of a party of visitors. Preparation also includes the selection of particular exhibits or rooms. As already noted, it is far more profitable to enjoy an hour or an hour and a half's concentrated viewing of a few galleries, than to attempt to visit a whole museum or a bewildering succession of museums and buildings. The selection should be based on a theme related to teaching in school, or college or evening class, and integrated with this, or else related to previous experience.

The best moment for the visit is about half way through a study project, when the children or students have some familiarity with the subject and its vocabulary, so that they are not both visiting the collections and struggling with the subject for the first time, a demanding process for the hardiest of adults. If possible the visitors, especially if young children, should be allowed to handle some objects from the collections. This form of direct contact brings the greatest rewards. A few moments spent in handling objects are worth as much as hours of viewing. The wide recognition of this has meant that many museums now have small special collections for this purpose and a room, where they can be used under adequate control. This satisfies the desire to handle and reduces the risk of damage to important exhibits.

On arrival in the gallery most children are somewhat overwhelmed and one of the best means of directing their attention, as well as of giving them a good chance to experience the exhibits is the provision of a work-sheet or some activity to pursue. This need not be of a formal nature and should not lead to reading of labels instead of looking at objects. Very often some blank sheets of paper for drawing form the best work-sheets. Some museum educationists do not like these forms of aid, because they are liable to become an end in themselves and to mar the true purpose of a visit. However they do form a very convenient method of directing the children's efforts in the museum and of providing a basis for follow-up work in school afterwards. Work-sheets provoke questions and discussion, and so provide a far more valuable vehicle for imparting knowledge than the formal lecture given in a classroom atmosphere with children sitting in rows.

Some museum services provide objects on loan, so that they may be kept in school and handled or seen regularly by the children. These services are usually financed by a local education authority and are linked closely with its policies. The objects are loaned for a term or half a term, thus enabling the teacher to make the fullest use of them, and the children to become well acquainted with the nature of the material and to learn to respect and like it. A good picture hung in the classroom becomes a familiar background, so that the children learn to appreciate the enrichment and enjoyment of living that can be gained from having fine objects as a normal part of the background to life.

As an obligation to the public and to the education of children, most museums are giving critical consideration to their display policy and to their publications. A very few museums are obliged to maintain an immutable display from the terms of some benefaction. Some curators do not wish to tread into the frenzied world of fashionable display trends and temporary exhibitions; they prefer to follow a steady programme of research and of the publication of more serious academic works. However, most curators sympathize with the movement towards more inviting, vivid and informative displays of exhibits, where the visitor feels comfortable and welcome. Reappraisal of the layout of exhibits and of their labelling has led to the use of simpler, more direct and enjoyable methods. Short and direct, the language and composition of good labels makes them intelligible and pleasant for all. Special labels for children are not really required, especially when a sound mind with a good grasp of language and of the subject in hand has prepared the standard ones.

Many museums—but again not enough—are publishing well-illustrated and authoritative booklets and notes, which are invaluable for preparation, viewing of exhibits and for follow-up. In addition, museums are publishing cheap but good quality reproductions of pictures, posters and manuscript material. If these are so priced that most children can purchase them, they are extremely important as reminders of a visit or reference works. They form something of the collections, which the visitor can take away with him and which will remind him of the pleasant time he experienced. This is a very important factor in promoting museum visits and in making visitors feel that the museum is theirs and that they can have a part in it.

There have been two further consequences of the increase in volume and scope of museum educational work.

First, a demand has arisen for the provision of out-of-school, holiday activity centres or clubs in museums. In response, many museums and art galleries have created studio space where children can meet regularly during free time to enjoy competitions, quizzes and various kinds of creative activity such as modelling, painting or drawing. Club leaders demand a reasonable standard of interest and knowledge, so that the child who is not really interested soon drops out. Extra staff are recruited, so that relief for the main education staff can be provided, and so that fresh ideas and energies can be employed. Very often student teachers, married women

27

teachers or arts-trained people wanting part-time employment, are glad to take up work of this nature and enjoy the stimulation of working with the children. In the case of natural-history museums these activities have been further extended by the formation of nature trails in neighbouring parks or countryside. In these ways the museums have played a fuller part in the lives of the children and the children have found the museums more enjoyable and enriching places to spend time, to the great benefit of all.

Secondly, there has been a rising demand for the provision of similar facilities for parents. The children's interest and enthusiasm have drawn their mothers and fathers into taking an interest in museums and to enjoying the great wealth of cultural treasures they provide. To meet this demand, museum staff have organized concerts, lectures, discussion groups and film shows over and above the normal extent of such programmes. This movement has also formed part of a more extensive movement to provide education for adults in a world in which industrial and commercial processes are becoming increasingly mechanized, so that less time is required for earning a living and more time is available for recreation and the enjoyment of hobbies. Other factors that have influenced this situation are the greatly improved facilities for cheap travel to important cultural centres provided by the holiday industry and the expansion in production and distribution of reasonably priced and extensively illustrated books.

Museums make another important contribution by allowing their staff to organize and give lectures in courses run by local education authorities, both within and outside the museum. Special evening occasions are organized for those attending such courses, and loan exhibitions of museum material are mounted. National museums are running extensive programmes of high-standard loan exhibitions which are available to a wide range of educational institutions and which form a good, controlled means of bringing the collection to people in remote areas. Museums also organize symposia and discussion groups for students and the public. In these and many other ways museums are helping the adult as well as the child to enjoy and profit from the great cultural heritage which he possesses.

It may seem that much of all this great effort in museum education is of a rather formal nature and not compatible with enjoyment. However, a moment's reflection will show that a principal aim of a museum educator is to lead both adults and children to enjoy acquiring knowledge through a love of fine things or of high scientific achievement. This is not a painful process in which progress is only made as a result of coercion and of threats of dire punishment. The professional supervision and advice of the museum education staff and curators is essential to the proper fulfilment of such programmes, but what could be pleasanter than sharing and gaining learning with others when surrounded by fine things which transmit knowledge eternally?

Examination of the reasons why a community or a nation should bother to spend money in conserving collections inevitably leads to this one conclusion; to pass on knowledge and appreciation of their excellence and importance. This form of education involves many disciplines for children as well as for adults. Amongst these is social discipline itself. A visit to a museum or the use of study collections demands correct social behaviour and a reasoned approach. The visitor or student who uses the gallery as a place to practise extremes of political protest by mutilating exhibits or to pursue nefarious private practices such as drug taking or merely as a comfortable place in which to fall asleep all day, every day, are very soon directed to pursue such matters elsewhere. Children's energies have to be channelled so that they do not intrude on other people's enjoyment of the displays and so that they gain a proper respect for the exhibits. It is of no use whatsoever if the teacher or leader of the children's party slopes off to the local drinking house or restaurant. Trouble is almost certain to ensue, if his children have any character or spirit; or they may well slope off themselves.

Further, by leading adults and children to experience museum collections educators are awakening and developing their critical faculties. At the very least, the child or adult reacts by liking or disliking the object on display. The educator can build on this by investigating the reasons for it. Through question and argument the visitor can be shown that his attitude is a purely emotional one or that there are sound reasons for it. Perhaps the object under study is of a poor design for its function, or a painter's concepts are too extreme to be readily comprehensible. All the time the visitor's reactions are being probed and directed, so that his mental eyes are opened as afresh, not just to knowledge but to a critical awareness of the objects surrounding him in the museum. The growth of his sensitivity to his general surroundings is thus encouraged. No longer will he walk down a street blinkered to everything except the clock or the traffic-lights which immediately direct his steps. Instead he will examine buildings, cars, town layouts, all his surroundings with a well-informed, critical mind.

For those who live in recently built estates of concrete tower blocks, concrete pathways, concrete houses unrelieved by good design, play areas, sufficient garden space or even attractively coloured doorways, in estates where horizons are bound by expressions of the overstrained public administrative purse, the museum or art gallery opens up fresh horizons, new worlds and offers a vital and enlivening experience. For children of parents living in a small apartment on the twelfth or higher floor of a tower block, there is little stimulus or outlet for any cultural energies and interests. The world must be a dull bleak place, governed by the efficient functioning of the lift or escalator. For these children the stimulation of a museum or gallery visit is of fundamental educational importance.

And so the most important reason for making the best use of museum collections—stimulation; stimulation to learn and to enjoy life more richly, to know more of oneself and of others. Such stimulation comes through contact with objects, with the creative work of artists and craftsmen, with the achievements of great minds in science and technology and with the products of history. Nothing has replaced and nothing will replace the impact of the real object, the experience of seeing, or better still of handling, the actual piece made by a great artist or used by someone many years ago. Expression of the thrill that this experience gives is seen in the wonderful and varied work produced by children and by students, in their willingness to come back and find out more or to go on elsewhere to discover further worlds of learning. Adults enjoy an enrichment of living and a broadening of horizons. So, like the great stained windows of a beautiful building, museums and galleries pour light of many colours and intensities in which we revel and grow, to our delight and to that of others.

An economic role for museums in the developing countries

3

The following represents part of our work at the National Museum—social and economic activities that museums in the developing countries must undertake to avoid the risk of being considered useless institutions, isolated from the national life.

THE FIRST OBSTACLE

In Africa, and more particularly in black Africa, the importance of museums is not always too well understood, so that—apart from the general scarcity of material resources—museum projects are often put off because other activities are considered more important.

In fact, a museum in Africa can be another sort of school. Ordinary schools give the basic education, museums provide an important supplement.

However, they strive to educate entertainingly. This often misleads well-intentioned people into thinking that they only offer entertainment, and not a different form of education. We remember a time in parts of Africa when parents would not send their children to school; mass vaccination was accepted only after a long struggle; and we all remember the objections to using audiovisual methods and television in education. There have always and everywhere been people to deplore the 'waste' on pure research—which has in fact led to nearly all the astounding discoveries and inventions of the present age.

There is as much difference between the school of the past, where the acquisition of knowledge depended largely on the instructive value of the cane, and the dynamic school of today, attractive and efficient; as between the old museum, designed for the erudite and the dilettante, and the wide open museum of today, conceived to serve the greatest possible number of people.

There are tenacious prejudices, overt and otherwise, which must be overcome in the developing countries, by giving museums a social and even economic role.

The word 'economic' may surprise but, as will be seen below, its use can easily be justified in the case of an African museum.

THE DILEMMA

The problem was to create a museum lively enough to attract the people and be at the same time educative. It had to interest the ordinary people, those most in need of help. A museum for the illiterate? Why not? At the risk of being misunderstood, we decided to concentrate on what we thought was most needed, to attempt a compromise that would satisfy the educated without boring the illiterate. We believe we have succeeded. At all costs, there must be nothing sacred about the museum, and if the approval of the educated visitor was precious, that of the uneducated was indispensable.

We expected criticism. From the outset,

P. Toucet is Curator at the National Museum of Niger.

General view of the National Museum.

The wood and ivory carver with his three apprentices.

The master smith (left) has two apprentices:
his son (right) and a man from another ethnic
group.

The leather-worker and his apprentice.

however, the government and the French technical assistance experts fully understood what we hoped to do, and though, from the opening, the population came *en masse*, it still remained for us to convince the sceptics.

Fortunately, we had the backing of specialists from the Monuments and Museums Section of the Unesco Department of Culture and from the International Council of Museums (ICOM). Unesco also supplied us with considerable material aid, and it is only right that I should express here the gratitude we feel.

What follows may surprise more than one reader.

MUSEUMS AND NATIONAL UNITY

The independent African nations, now masters of their own destinies as far as any country can be in this world of economic interdependence, must ensure their own survival and development.

Plans are drawn up, discussed, approved. Priorities are accorded. As financial resources are always inadequate in relation to needs, a demand for funds to build a museum may seem highly absurd to realistic minds. Yet it merits consideration, and may find justification on grounds other than the normal artistic and scientific concerns of museums.

The history, ethnography and geography of African nations is far from homogeneous. They need to affirm their individuality and cohesion. Their full participation in international life began only a few decades ago; their governments know full well that, to blend together in a collective consciousness the ethnographic and historical roots of their peoples this will be a long and arduous task that must receive full priority.

How could we have a policy coherent at home as well as abroad, beyond our inherited European-made boundaries, without first forging a voluntary union that would allow the new State to take root? How bring a better way of life and protection under a common flag to men and women scattered over vast territories? How convert ancestral enemies into brothers? In a word: how create a national unity to withstand the disintegrating forces that threaten much older nations?

It is already some time since Mr de Varine-Bohan, Director of ICOM, reported that the first country to use a museum effectively to back a government in promoting national unity was Niger, followed closely by Mexico.

What the National Museum can do for national unity is of course just a drop in the ocean. But since it was set up, it has modestly done what it can. With loving care, it has revealed to people the thousand objects that make up their daily life, a veritable ethnographic treasure, not on account of their material value, but because they are authentic. Faithfully and with respect, we have reconstructed every form of housing from distant and diverse parts of the country, so that anyone can see and study them without having to travel immense distances. Better still, the modern buildings we have put up at the museum are based architecturally on traditional *banco* constructions, in an effort to show that Niger potentially has an architecture to satisfy its needs, which only needs to be developed and adapted to present requirements.

Trying yet another means, the museum has brought craftsmen together from the four corners of Niger. This was done not only to conserve the traditional techniques, but mainly—since 1959—to allow Zarma and Tuareg, Songhay and Hausa, Beri-beri and Peul to work hand-in-hand together to crystallize national unity—a laboratory demonstration to show that national unity was both wanted and possible.

ROLE IN THE NATIONAL ECONOMY

Museums, present and future, can, to a greater or lesser extent, play an economic role in developing countries, and this in two ways: through tourists and through artisans.

Museums everywhere are increasingly attracting tourists. To make the most of this phenomenon in Africa, museums must be designed to give the tourist—who usually has not the time to make long trips into the interior—as varied and complete an idea as possible of the country he is visiting.

With this in mind, the museum of Niamey tried to present, in synthesis, the vast country of Niger. The extensive park contains dwellings representing the different ethnic groups, the nomad and the settled. Builders had sometimes to come 1,000 kilometres and more to put up these traditional dwellings. Tents and huts contain the usual, everyday furniture and utensils. This open-air museum, made still more live by the craftsmen working there, has so natural an atmosphere that it does not seem like a museum at all. Niger ceremonial and battle clothes, on revolving mannequins, are displayed in a nearby pavilion.

Thus the tourist can very rapidly get the human picture: artisans from all the ethnic groups, the traditional techniques, the way things are actually made, the various types of dwelling, the splendid traditional costumes.

This ethnographic view of Niger can be followed up by a visit to a zoo which has specimens of practically all the country's fauna. In pools or cages of proverbial cleanliness, the animals live peacefully without seeming to miss too much the often hostile bush that is close by. In some eight hectares of rather wild countryside, the intrepid tourist can photograph giraffes, buffaloes, antelopes, ostriches and so on in the bush, to show his friends when he gets home. This may seem funny, but psychologically there is undoubtedly an attraction—and the tourist, in any case, does run the risk of a peck from an ostrich or a charge (quickly checked by the keepers) from a nostalgic buffalo. Finally, the fish of the river Niger can be viewed in a small aquarium.

It is easy to see what pleasure tourists take in visiting a museum like this; and it is hardly necessary to point out what a source of revenue they represent today.

Secondly, handicrafts: many museums throughout the world have craft workshops which not only do invaluable ethnographic research, but constitute an appreciable source of income. In African museums, they are especially valuable, and we feel our experience may be useful to museums wishing to start or extend one.

When we first installed artisans in our open-air museum, the main purpose was ethnographical: to preserve traditional techniques and let visitors see them. But to be able to allow them to continue, we had to sell what they made. A gift enabled us to set up a first stand. It soon became too small for the number of buyers. A further, even more generous gift, allowed us to construct the present stand, which has so far proved adequate.

The total of sales in the first year was a few hundred thousand francs. By 1969, the number of craftsmen had increased from fifteen to eighty, sixty of them working at the museum; and sales rose to 12 million francs. For 1970 they should be 18–20 million francs, as sales for the first half of 1969 practically doubled in 1970.

Consequently, we gave work to a large number of craftsmen: this enhanced their standing; preserved traditional skills; gave new life to the museum; made a modest contribution to economic development; and found additional funds for the museum. It should be remembered that the craftsmen are not employees, but piece workers. They are free to come and go as they please, but find it better to remain at the museum (the first fifteen are still there).

A price must be paid for these results. The craftsmen must be the best available, selected strictly on merit. They must learn to respect agreed prices and delivery dates. Objects must be examined one by one, and anything badly made or ethnographically false rejected. A catalogue is necessary to simplify foreign sales. Prices must be based on real cost of production, so as to protect both maker and buyer.

In short, tourists and handicrafts give a

Songhay weaver and Zerma apprentice.

Potter and apprentice (neither wheel nor kiln).

Temporary open-air school for girls.

Teaching the young the alphabet.

museum an economic role and an ability to earn that defuses so much of the 'common-sense' criticism which insinuates that museums are a useless extravagance in a developing country.

CRAFT TRAINING

The reader must inevitably draw the conclusion we did: the museum itself must train good craftsmen. Here, in simple terms, is exactly what we did.

A large number of boys were affected, one way or another, by our educational and social activities (see below). We selected those who seemed most anxious to learn a craft.

To be selected, they had to have attended primary school up to school-certificate standard. Courses are arranged for them by the museum's master-craftsmen, who explain in detail how the raw material is transformed into an object of both ethnographic and commercial value. The boys literally bombard the craftsmen with questions. Each is assigned to the craft which best suits his temperament and manual skills.

The apprentices then work under the best and most responsible of our craftsmen, the arrangement being made by mutual agreement between apprentice and master. All apprenticeship expenses are borne by the museum. Constantly rising sales allow us to recruit about twenty annually.

Various deeply rooted prejudices had to be overcome. In many African countries, craftsmen have always been looked down on. Even if the boys, desperately needing to find some way to earn a living, were quite happy to become craftsmen (especially seeing how well off are those working at the museum), the parents, or some of them, were more than dubious.

It is silly and rather mad that men capable of weaving, forging, carving or moulding such splendid things should be looked down on by people incapable of making anything with their hands.

Our museum is proud of having helped to put the crafts back in their rightful place in Niger. The proof?—eight years ago, we could not find children to train; today we have more candidates than we can accommodate, because now we have not only to train them but, once trained, find work for them through the museum.

HELPING THE YOUNG UNEMPLOYED

Many boys and girls fail to find work in the towns. Some failed to get a place in the State schools. Others finished primary school (with or without certificate) but still could not find work. This happens in many developing countries, because more are born than there are jobs—public or private—available.

Accordingly, many remain illiterate. Others, who were fortunate enough to go to school, little by little forget what they have learned; and many, unfortunately, having had a State education, simply turn their backs on the land and hate the idea of learning a trade. Here, as elsewhere, the white-collar job retains its attraction.

These quite obviously represent an important social problem, which the State fully realizes and tries to solve with the help of various *ad hoc* arrangements.

Our museum felt that it could help, and said so to these boys and girls. Over two hundred responded, at which figure we reluctantly had to stop.

Having neither the funds nor the resources for an educational and social operation, we appealed to various organizations. Their help has enabled us to provide a kind of education, effective if unorthodox, and which has the merit of arousing and maintaining interest.

With the help of others, here is what we have managed to do.

Monday. Legends, stories and historical narratives, introduced and commented by one of the Niger Radio-Television staff. The children discuss what they have heard, and re-tell the stories, much to everyone's pleasure. These are recorded, and broadcast by Radio Niger.

41

Tuesday. Practical hygiene and first-aid course, given by the Niger Red Cross.

Wednesday. Introduction to the spoken arts and the dance, music appreciation, drawing and free painting (experiments in collective expression), by the Franco-Niger Cultural Centre.

Thursday. Educational films shown by the American Cultural Centre. The subject of each film is explained to the children beforehand, and afterwards freely discussed by them.

Friday. An instructor from the Training and Education Centre teaches boys various do-it-yourself techniques that need a minimum of tools.

Saturday. Civics: talks also on traditional techniques and handicrafts by the master-craftsmen.

The afternoons are devoted to reading and writing classes for illiterate children, given by a teacher assigned to the museum by the Minister of Education, and according to a curriculum prepared by the Institute of Education.

There are as many girls as boys. Their courses are more conventional. In the mornings, three teachers, one employed by the museum and two from 'Volunteers for Progress', give lessons at the levels laid down by the Institute of Education. In the afternoons, they learn practical home economics, child care, hygiene and first aid.

With help from others and without special funds, the museum has thus been able to provide this educational and social service for the young unemployed. Lack of financial or other means is not reason enough for doing nothing, although it would be going too far to say that all this has been easy. Here, as elsewhere, the will and determination are necessary.

ADULT LITERACY

The audio-visual pavilion we were able to construct with United States aid is a great asset. In the mornings it is used for the teaching just mentioned. In the afternoons it becomes a school, like any other, for illiterate children. In the evenings, courses are given in collaboration with the Literacy Board, for craftsmen (some of whom come straight from the bush), gardeners, cleaners, labourers or any other illiterate staff of the museum.

These courses, attentively followed by about sixty adults, some fifty years old or more, rid them of an additional complex: their feeling of inferiority to apprentices who can already read, write and count.

This literacy campaign may help us to atone for a fault: having taken so long to undertake it.

There is nothing particularly original in all that is described above, nothing that could not easily be done by anyone else. Perhaps that is its importance. Competent and well-meaning specialists often offer splendid plans and advice to museums in the developing countries, without taking any real account of what they can actually do. Outside help can decide whether or not a museum will be built at all. It is still necessary to remember that there will also be the cost of running it.

But the final purpose is always the same: to make something else of a museum than a temple of art or science.

R. Subramanian

Science, museums and planetaria

4

Museum work was given a new impetus in India about fifteen years ago by the great surge of interest in science, technology and industry. National research and development laboratories for chemistry, electrochemistry, physics, metallurgy, biochemistry, medicine, fuel technology, mining, leather technology and so on had been established in several cities. Existing agriculture and forestry institutes expanded their work to cover modern methods of farming and the design of newer and better tools and implements. An atomic energy centre was set up in Bombay and its reactors were fully operational. Aircraft, machine-tool and other heavy-engineering industries were started. Science museums were a natural corollary to all this. India already had rich museums of long standing devoted to art, archaeology, numismatics, botany, zoology, anthropology and geology, and display methods were catching up with modern trends. But, for one reason or another, the physical sciences and technology had hitherto been largely ignored.

K. S. Krishnan, Director of the National Physical Laboratory, Delhi, was receiving letters daily from educational institutions in and around Delhi and from groups of students in other parts of India for permission to visit the laboratory, its departments, library and workshops. There was great interest, among students and public alike, in science and technology. Demonstrating the

peculiar properties of liquified air, for example (a piece of rubber dipped in the liquid became completely brittle and could be broken into pieces like a twig), fascinated thousands; or the quartz clock, accurate to a tiny fraction of a second; or the magnification possible with an electron microscope. Hence, probably, the director's decision to set up the nucleus of a science museum which could later be shifted elsewhere when enough experience had been gained regarding types of exhibits, presentation techniques and associated educational activities.

The present author was appointed scientific officer on the science-museum project at the time (1956) after studying in Europe and the United States under an American Philosophical Society fellowship and a Fulbright travel grant for studies at the Johns Hopkins University, and the Smithsonian Institution. Visits were made to science museums, planetaria and children's museums.

In Delhi, for science exhibits and for experiments with display and animation techniques, 6,000 square feet were provided on a ground floor and mezzanine, together with office space and secretarial help. To start with, thirty exhibits were set up to explain the work of various laboratories on behalf of science and industry; a varied collection of minerals and ores, gifts made to the late Prime Minister, Pandit Jawaharlal Nehru, during his visits abroad, were also exhibited (including a fine quartz crystal conglomeration, with dozens of quartz units presenting clear-cut faces). A closed-circuit television

R. Subramanian is Curator and Technical Director, Birla Planetarium and Astronomy Gallery, Calcutta.

set was used for an educational exhibit, as was also a four-line twenty-extension telephone exchange (a gift from one of the East European countries), after some modification.

An assistant with an M. Sc. in physics and electronics, a physics graduate with some experience in the fabrication of scientific equipment and in popularizing and teaching science, and an energetic and enterprising young technician were also engaged. With this staff to assist, visits and lectures were arranged for the public, and for student and farming groups.

The television unit, as expected, proved the greatest attraction. The telephone exchange fascinated students and children. Two added lines could be dialled and operated by visitors, and they never missed an opportunity.

It was found in general that when accompanied by a guide, visitors carefully examined the exhibits, charts and flow diagrams but, when left to themselves, they skipped many of them. The glistening specimens like malachite, azurite and agate caught their fancy—no doubt, the beautiful quartz conglomeration kept them wondering how nature managed to create such fine crystals of hard material—but not the rest of the minerals. As an explanatory exhibit to the mineral collections, crystallographic models were prepared, with thick coloured paper fixed on stiff wire netting. These interested some by their geometrical shapes, and others (college and university students) on academic grounds; for the benefit of the latter, further models were made, using perspex to show the X, Y and GT cuts of quartz.

In 1956, a large 'India and Science' exhibition was set up to coincide with a session of the Unesco General Conference held in Delhi. Some of the science exhibits, suitably modified, were afterwards shifted to the museum. One was a surge generator, in which sparks flashed spectacularly as an increased voltage broke down the insulation gap. The first quartz clock unit assembled by the lab-

oratory's Time and Frequency Department was also transferred to the museum. Using a language as simple as possible, the guide explained the mechanism and working of the quartz clock but was never wholly reassured by the hesitant nod of the visitor. A Lissajous pendulum drew fine symmetrical patterns through the sand flowing out of the nozzle at the bottom of the conical container when released diagonally. A Hipp's pendulum was also fabricated, with the typical butterfly escapement, and every time the oscillation fell below the critical amplitude, the tongue was kicked and completed the electrical circuit, energizing the electromagnet, and so increasing the amplitude again. A lamp flashed each time the amplitude was restored. The principle is simple, but critical adjustments had to be made to keep the pendulum working flawlessly—as we realized before achieving full success. Other exhibits explained Faraday's disc, the jumping spiral, sparks through Wimshurst's machine, magnetic lines of force, and so on. In each case the design had to be sturdy enough to allow constant handling by visitors and at the same time be simple and elegant.

The museum borrowed ideas from the Unesco travelling science exhibition *Energy and its Transformations* set up in Delhi in 1956. It has since received a gift of another Unesco travelling exhibition (*Our Senses and the Knowledge of the World*) which includes instruments; several working exhibits, neatly and elegantly designed, to teach the principles governing vision, perception, sound, smell, touch and so on; and a set of panels with illustrations and crisply worded explanations. Several scientific firms had given the instruments to Unesco as gifts, and various institutions and professors had co-operated in preparing the handbook. The exhibition had travelled widely before reaching Delhi and some parts had inevitably been damaged. These were repaired at the museum. Primary colours, colour mixing, colours of the spectrum, the persistence of vision, background, illusions concerning the intensity of colour, stereoscopic vision, the poloroid camera, disc recording, sound patterns of the vibrating tuning fork, microscopes of different types, telescopes and binoculars were illustrated in exhibits which visitors (mostly school groups) were encouraged to use or operate. The results were very encouraging.

Unesco provided the services of an expert museologist, a six-month fellowship for an Indian graduate to study museum techniques in Europe, and $5,000 worth of equipment. The expert W. T. O'Dea, then Keeper of the Science Museum, London, arrived in Delhi early in 1957. As he told the Delhi paper *The Statesman* on arrival: 'The object of the museum will be not only to interest people in science but to let them do things. We have left behind the old conception of museums. Modern museums are educational institutions where visitor participation is invited. The greatest benefit from the science museum will be in correcting Indians' disinclination to go in for jobs that are not entirely white collar. India needs a number of technologists and a lot of potential is wasted here.'

On Mr O'Dea's advice, the layout was reorganized. The closed-circuit television unit was so placed that visitors could see themselves televised through a mirror reflecting the television screen. Part of the Unesco funds were used on an automatic, two-language English and Hindi talking exhibit, set up near the entrance, and consisting of a series of transparencies with a map of India engraved on perspex. This exhibit clearly demonstrated the value of animation, and the importance of using the local language. Everyone felt quite at home, since the exhibit was operated simply by pressing a (sturdy) push button. Even poorly educated manual workers frequently initiated friends and relatives by inviting them in and pressing the button to turn on the Hindi commentary. Such exhibits would be extremely useful in science and other museums all over India.

The expert also went to Pilani, some 200 kilometres from Delhi, to advise on a mu-

seum started by V. P. Beri under the Birla Education Trust. Apart from their industries, Birla have set up several educational, scientific and charitable endowments. Pilani itself has science and engineering colleges, and an internationally famed institute on the lines of the Massachusetts Institute of Technology. Mr Beri, for the first time in India, had introduced working models employing several animation techniques (mostly made locally) and dioramas.

Birla also donated a palatial house and land at Calcutta for another museum, described in some detail below.

To mark the centenary celebrations of the engineer-statesman, M. Visvesvaraya, an industrial society was formed in Bangalore. It collected donations and erected a building near the archaeology and natural history museum. It contains four floors, a total of 40,000 square feet, with a basement (2,000 square feet) for a workshop. The museum was handed over to the Council of Scientific and Industrial Research which facilitates coordination with the museums at Calcutta and at Bangalore.

After a period of study in Europe on the Unesco fellowship, the author's return to the museum in Delhi coincided with the start of the space era: the launching of the first Sputnik by the Soviet Union.

The fast-moving developments in space technology brought in visitors with more and more inquiries on this topic and on the composition of the universe, the planets, moon and stars. A medium-sized planetarium was set up in the laboratory campus, with a gallery, displaying star fields, planets, views of the moon and the twelve zodiacal signs, made to glow against the darkness by the radiation from ultra-violet lamps. The projection unit was a gift from the East German Government and was set up under the dome, with accommodation for from thirty-five to forty persons. The arc-shaped astronomy gallery was linked to the planetarium, so that one group could observe the exhibits shining under black light while the other attended the

Children looking through a 2-inch refractor telescope.

Beautiful patterns of a sand pendulum delight the schoolchildren.

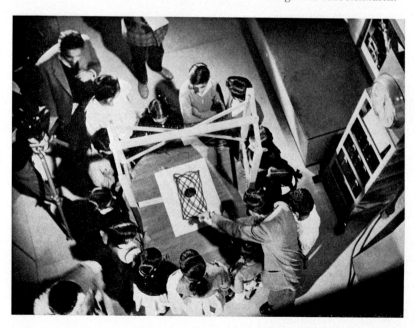

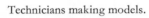

Working model showing orbit of Sputnik I.

Technicians making models.

Model of Branca's wheel fabricated in the workshops.

Radioactivity model: as the disc rotates, the minerals move towards the Geiger counter and luminous pulses and 'tick-ticks' flash from the instruments on the left.

Historical equipment that illustrates the developments of science is essential for museums: early vacuum pumps (gifts from the Science Museum, London).

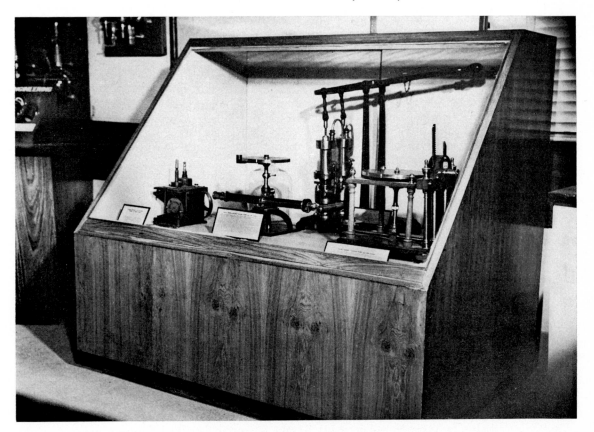

demonstration lecture under the dome. As both these required darkness and closed doors, air-conditioners were fitted to the windows.

The science museum itself received various gifts from the Science Museum, London: hour-glasses (sand clock), early spring-driven clocks, Joule's heat experiment replica, replica of Leuvenhoek's hand microscope, early Edison phonographs, early vacuum pumps, slides from photographs showing ancient time-keepers like oil lamps, nocturnals and so on. A working model of Sputnik I was also provided. Seeing the model in action, visitors could understand how an artificial satellite at a specific inclination to the plane of orbit of the earth could, in consecutive sightings from a particular place, appear to be moving across the sky in different directions. A working model of a two-stroke internal-combustion engine was prepared from drawings in a Unesco teaching-aid book. A drawing of the *Rocket* locomotive engine was studied section by section, and the various parts were fabricated in the workshop.

The museum next employed additional staff—scientific and technical assistants, an electrician, a photographer and a draftsman. Between 1957 and 1960 import restrictions were very severe. Indian industry had various supply difficulties. More and more animation items such as ratio reduction gears, time switches and so on had to be made locally. Sometimes powerful motors had to be used because noiseless smaller ones were not available. Certain relay contacts and micro-switches were just appearing in the market. We had some success in making our own electrical and electronic circuits. An elegantly designed working model of a uni-selector, for example, had preceded the telephone exchange exhibit. The visitor lifted the handset. Through a micro-switch, this lit a tiny lamp which, through reflection in a mirror, made the cut-out rear view of the telephone dial visible. Dialling switched on as many lights in a sequence as there were digits in the number. Putting back the handset operated the homing sector and brought the instrument to the starting point. Geiger counters with digital pulses and ticks were used to show the radioactivity of different minerals fixed on a rotating disc.

More working exhibits were gradually added to enhance historical perspective. The museum helped with science exhibitions in schools and colleges and began a sky observation programme in which the local Amateur Astronomical Association took part. News-sheets on scientific and astronomical topics were distributed to the schoolchildren.

At the request of the government, the author prepared a draft plan for a national science museum for the Indian capital. However, this project had to be postponed. As buildings were already available at Calcutta and Bangalore, activities shifted to these two centres. Part of the exhibits at the National Physical Laboratory were moved to other points.

A Birla project for a huge planetarium and astronomy gallery had already started in Calcutta, and the author moved there. The planetarium went into operation on 29 September 1962. With a hemispherical dome measuring 75 feet in its inner diameter it was the largest in Asia, and second only to the Moscow planetarium. It cost the Birla Education Trust 3 million rupees. Its purpose is to facilitate the study of astronomy, astrophysics and celestial mechanics, to develop an astronomy gallery and, in due course, to do research on astronomy in India in ancient times.

The circular hall accommodates 500 persons. Demonstrations are handled by the lecturer from the console near the entrance. A series of knobs and switches allow him to manipulate the instrument and to represent the true-to-nature artificial man-made starry sky on the inner surface of the dome. Auxiliary equipment includes the shooting-star projection unit, the working scale-model solar-system projection equipment, the projection unit to depict the zodiac and other constellation figures, the projectors for the network of astronomical reference circles, the artificial satellite projection unit, the projection system for the partial, total and annular eclipses. Sound is carried through a series of loudspeakers kept along the periphery just below the Calcutta skyline. Soft music fed from the control room pervades the auditorium through a loudspeaker kept hidden at the zenith position.

The technician at the control room feeds in the music and keeps a watch on the motors, relays, switches and transformers which energize the several units. On cue from the lecturer he also feeds in the rocket blast-off noise, the noise of the solar flares, or the clarion call of the cock at dawn.

Usually three or four new themes are designed and shown to the public during each period of from nine to twelve months, e.g. some aspect of the solar system; stars and galaxies; space travel. From time to time, mythological stories associated with the star patterns are included.

These programmes are given in three languages daily: Bengali (the local language), Hindi (the national language) and English (the link language); and occasionally in other languages: Oriya, Tamil and Gujarati. An admission fee is charged, with special rates for student groups. Five 45-minute demonstration lectures are given daily. On Saturdays there is one extra programme; on Sundays, three. During the last seven or eight years, over thirty-five topics in astronomy have been explained to a total of 2.75 million visitors, from all parts of India and abroad. Attendances have progressively increased every year.

The planetarium also gives graded programmes for different school groups; 10–12 years, 12–14 and 14–16. For each of these graded demonstration lectures (given in Bengali, Hindi and English), ten schools are invited to send fifty students each. The programmes cover the familiar star patterns; the seasons of the year; the path of the sun as seen from different latitudes and at the poles;

the solar system; the Milky Way and so on. The general and school programmes now invariably contain numerous references to rockets, artificial satellites, spacecraft and probes.

In the circular gallery surrounding the dome, there are telescopic views of celestial bodies and star fields; busts of famous astronomers and thinkers; murals depicting the planets according to Hindu mythology (*Navagrahas*); and marble slabs with inscriptions from the *Vedas* and *Upanishads*. These have a particular charm for Indian visitors, who listen with a religious zeal to talks on the vastness of space and the arrangement of the universe. Through the co-operation of the United States Information Service, exhibits about space achievements are periodically added; the latest is a scale model of the powerful Saturn-V rocket used for boosting astronauts on the way to the moon. Space exhibits concerning Russian achievements have also been added through the co-operation of the Russian Consulate. A fine scale model of the great radiotelescope at Manchester was presented by the British High Commissioner.

A unique feature of the planetarium is its annual evening course in astronomy, which is given completely free of charge. Its purpose is to create or maintain an interest in astronomy. Its twenty-three topics include the history of astronomy, observational atronomy, celestial mechanics, astrophysics, origin and age of the solar system and of the universe, galaxies and the depths of space. Usually 150 enrol for each course and they divide into groups of fifty each. Each group receives one 1-hour lecture each week. The course is followed by demonstrations with astronomical instruments. Film shows are included. A sky observation programme using a 3-inch refractor is arranged, sometimes by the planetarium and sometimes in conjunction with the museum. These courses, programmes and activities arouse much enthusiasm and interest e.g. an astronomical expedition consisting of an evening-course student and the author who, equipped with

This complex and delicate astronomical
projection instrument, containing more than
29,000 parts, is the heart of the Birla Planetarium,
Calcutta. (Photo: Studio Orient, Calcutta.) ▶

Birla Planetarium, Calcutta: established by the
Birla Education Trust in 1962, it is the only
one of its kind in India, the largest in Asia and
the second largest in the world. It is fully air-
conditioned. (Photo: Studio Orient, Calcutta.)

Birla Planetarium, Calcutta; evening course ▶
in astronomy: the Chairman, Planetarium
Advisory Committee and Minister for Social
Welfare, Government of India, Dr Phulrenu
Guha, addressing students.

Central Museum, Birla Institute of Technology and Science, Pilani: established in 1954, it is the premier technological museum in India. (Photo: Studio New Light, New Delhi.)

Central Museum, Pilani: general view from the water pool situated in the middle of the display areas. (Photo: Studio New Light, New Delhi.)

Central Museum, Pilani: part of the metallurgy
section. (Photo: Studio New Light, New Delhi.)

telescopes, cameras and stands, flew to a point about 400 miles from Calcutta, to study and photograph a rare annular solar eclipse.

The planetarium hopes to set up a popular observatory, and a research branch for the study of ancient Indian astronomy. Relevant literature is being collected.

Various institutions have been helped to set up planetaria and arrange astronomy and science exhibitions. Special programmes are prepared for National Children's Day in November. The staff give radio talks and publish articles in magazines and newspapers. Publicity is obtained through news items and advertisements in local papers and in *What's on in Calcutta* (a local fortnightly). A commercial firm was permitted to reproduce the *Navagrahas* (with due acknowledgement) in its calendars, one way of attracting religious-minded Indians to visit the planetarium. A coloured folder on the *Navagrahas* is to be published later. Postcards are available showing the projection instrument and views of the building, together with a brochure that discusses astronomy and gives details about the complex projection equipment.

A survey was recently made. Over 100 persons of different age groups, status and interests were each interviewed for about half an hour by an enthusiastic museologist (C. V. Nageswara) who was associated with the planetarium for a short period. The results will help to improve programmes in the light of the reactions and views of visitors.

The author had the privilege of representing India at the seminar on Museums and the New Public, organized in Warsaw and Cracow by Unesco, the Polish National Commission for Unesco and ICOM, which discussed the changes that have been taking place since the Second World War and the need to assess the requirements, demands and reactions of the new public. This trip to Europe also permitted visits to the planetarium at Vienna; to the Euginides Planetarium and Science Museum at Athens; to the planetarium and galleries of the Deutsches Museum at Munich; the Polytechnic Museum at Warsaw; the university containing the equipment used by Copernicus and the planetarium, astronomy gallery and observation platforms at Katowice. These visits and discussions with museum colleagues have been immensely fruitful and provided ideas that are gradually being applied in the planetarium and galleries at Calcutta.

The Birla Central Museum at Pilani offers Indian industry a permanent show-case to illustrate its continuing progress and keep people of all ages and backgrounds informed about new trends and developments in technology and industry. Founded in 1954, it is the premier technological museum of India. The exhibits, working models, and dioramas have been prepared by the staff in its own workshop—an excellent way, incidentally, of developing local skills. The emphasis has been on do-it-yourself type exhibits that invite the visitor to participate. The sheer elegance of the presentation and surroundings is perhaps unrivalled in India. The galleries cover ten main subjects in an area of about 26,000 square feet: engineering, metallurgy, transport, space, chemistry, textiles, agriculture, mining, arms, pictures. The museum includes a large-scale underground coal-mine exhibit.

Recorded music, fountains, a pool centrally situated under the bridge, murals and motifs and the general décor of the galleries are pleasantly relaxing. The museum is open, free, six hours a day six days a week. Guided tours are led by trained staff, and the auditorium shows documentary films twice daily. Temporary exhibitions are put up from time to time on topics of current interest. The museum exhibits are kept constantly up to date. An additional block is shortly to be added, to house a new science section.

In Calcutta, the Birla Museum established in 1959 has by now become extremely popular, an essential venue for visitors to Calcutta as for local people and students: 86,000 visitors in 1960, 216,500 in 1967, with further increases since. The exhibits cover nuclear physics, power, iron and steel, copper, petroleum, mining, electricity, television, electronics, communications. The working models and dioramas are made in the museum's own modern electrical and mechanical workshops and art studio. During the formative years the museum was greatly helped by expert guidance and the training provided through fellowships.

The exhibits are accommodated on three floor levels and are composed of static models, working models, and in some cases actual objects, interspersed with neatly designed dioramas, suitably animated. The development of science and technology through the centuries is also woven into the fabric of the exhibition. The museum is open daily except on Mondays from 10 a.m. to 5 p.m., and admission is free except on Sundays. Scientific film shows are given daily, and television demonstrations by means of a closed-circuit unit. Popular lectures are arranged from time to time, and a growing science reference library is open to the public.

The museum provides extensive educational services outside its own premises. Mobile self-contained science exhibitions (*Our Familiar Electricity*, *Transformation of Energy*, *Light and Sound*) in trailer buses have visited over 400 points, covered some 20,000 km, and been seen by over 1 million people. Each consists of twenty-four working exhibits. This represents a unique and very successful mass-education experiment, worthy of emulation elsewhere. The museum has set up small regional science museums in rural schools at distances of 250–500 km from Calcutta. One, at Purulia (335 km from Calcutta), has been organized on a permanent basis.

Extensive school services are offered in the form of science demonstration lectures, hobby centres, and teacher-training programmes. A series of six demonstration lectures has been given in some 200 schools in Calcutta and 150 in rural parts. For this programme, exhibits are specially made in the museum to fit in with the school syllabus.

Twenty science hobby centres for students have been set up in Calcutta and in various districts. The teacher's training programmes show science teachers how to run the hobby centres and make demonstration exhibits. Other educational activities include a model-making competition and a science fair for students, which attract hundreds of ingeniously constructed entries.

The Bangalore museum has the advantage of having a building specifically designed as a museum, and was able to borrow from the experience gained at Pilani, since both museums were under the same administration. Handed over to the Council of Scientific and Industrial Research in 1962, the museum was formally inaugurated in 1965. Like the Pilani museum, it has its working models, animated dioramas, objects, panels, charts and historical background material.

Power, electrotechnology and popular science are the themes covered.

The museum is open every day, except Monday, from 10 a.m. to 5 p.m. Admission is free except on Sundays. There are regular guided tours and film shows. Demonstration lectures with models and films, on school-curriculum subjects are given at the museum (for city schools) and at rural schools. The museum offers popular science lectures and runs a hobby centre. A mobile science exhibition (*Water, the Fountain of Life*) in a trailer-bus follows the same pattern as in the other museums.

Bangalore is a much smaller city than Calcutta, but receives some 2,000 visitors a day, partly no doubt because the city is a tourist attraction all the year round. It has many historical monuments, palaces and parks. The great Krishnaraja Sagar Dam, with its aesthetically laid-out gardens, fountains and lighting is only 150 km away and a major tourist attraction. Bangalore also enjoys a pleasant climate throughout the year. The museum can be said to be naturally air-conditioned, which of course makes it easier for the visitors to observe and study the exhibits in detail.

Birla Museum, Calcutta: work at the Science Lobby Centre.

One of the mobile science exhibition units. Later versions use more spacious buses.

MOBILE SCIENCE EXHIBITION

Visvesvaraya Museum, Bangalore: general view
of the popular Science Gallery.
(Photo: G.K. Vale & Co., Bangalore.)

Visvesvaraya Museum, Bangalore: electrotechnology gallery model showing the working
of a telephone. (Photo: G.K. Vale & Co.,
Bangalore.)

The ICOM meetings held in India in 1969 saw something of the work of these museums in educating the public and students in rural areas in the local languages through demonstration lectures and small science museums and exhibitions. Delegates had met to discuss the question of setting up museum laboratories from which to develop basic exhibits for projects in developing countries, and were very impressed with what was being done in India.

The prospects for science education through museums and planetaria in India is fairly bright. Museums all over India, including the science and technological museums and planetaria, have had the rare privilege of having the advice of Dr Grace Morley who has always given unstintingly of her time. The author has also received great encouragement and help in his several projects from Dr C. Sivaramamurti, the internationally renowned archaeologist and historian, who is Director of the National Museum in New Delhi and Adviser to the Government of India, and President of the Indian National Committee for ICOM.

A good deal has been accomplished during the last fifteen years. Further plans now exist. A huge technological and industrial museum is likely to be set up very soon at Bombay. A multi-storey building is to be added as an annex to Birla Museum. A planetarium is to be built at the Visvesvaraya Museum (Bangalore). A memorial to Mahatma Gandhi at Vijayawada (about 600 km north-east of Madras) will consist of an amusement park, a science museum and a planetarium. The Birla planetarium will help to train lecturing staff and assist in the organization; it also gave technical assistance in the setting up of a medium-sized planetarium at Porbundar in Western India. It is hoped with reasonable confidence that similar facilities will become increasingly available, to spread the knowledge of science and technology among the population of this vast country.

Children and art

5

Children have no doubt been visiting museums with their parents and teachers ever since museums began to open their doors to the public during the eighteenth century, but programmes, services and facilities especially for them represent a twentieth-century development. The Brooklyn Children's Museum, the first in the world, was established in 1899 in an old mansion in New York. Its founder, Anna Billings Gallup, who had a truly missionary zeal, was indirectly responsible for at least four other children's museums—in Boston, Massachusetts (1914), Indianapolis, Indiana (1925), Hartford, Connecticut (1927) and Duluth, Minnesota (1930). Each foundation influenced other communities, and a new movement had started.

Our statistics are never quite up to date, but to my knowledge there are today at least a hundred children's museums in the United States and at least ten in other countries. More than half have been started since 1935. Most of the earlier ones were concerned with natural history, as the majority still are, but those founded in the last fifteen years are almost all devoted to art.

There has been an equally impressive growth in educational activities for children within established adult museums. George Fisk Comfort, one of the founders of the Museum of Fine Arts in Syracuse, N.Y., was considered a pioneer when, in 1901, he began

Louise Condit is Associate in Charge of the Junior Museum, the Metropolitan Museum of Art, New York.

inviting pupils to come with their teachers to hear talks on the exhibitions. In 1903, the Toledo Museum of Art in Ohio adopted a six-part educational plan with, first on the list, free drawing classes for children. The Metropolitan Museum of Art hired its first 'instructor' in 1908 to offer guidance in the galleries to 'teachers and scholars from the public schools'. The Worcester Art Museum in Massachusetts set aside a Children's Room in 1911. Here children (10 and older) could draw, read, work on picture puzzles, play gallery games, or listen to stories illustrated by slides and photographs. In 1914, the Boston Museum of Fine Arts offered, specially for children, an exhibition on Japan; the interest it aroused led to the establishment of the Children's Art Gallery in Boston in 1918. A two-day Meeting of Museum Instructors in America, called by the Metropolitan Museum of Art in 1915, was attended by thirty-eight representatives. In 1937 the Museum of Modern Art in New York established the Educational Project, with a Young People's Gallery offering exhibitions, artists' demonstrations, gallery visits, studio classes, and educational materials for member high schools. In 1941, when Eleanor Moore was writing *Youth and Museums*, she visited 106 museums in the United States and Canada considered outstanding for their educational work for young people (eighty-nine adult and seventeen children's museums): approximately half were art museums.

Later that same year (October 1941), the Metropolitan Museum of Art established its

Junior Museum, in five large galleries formerly occupied by plaster casts. Since 1957, it has occupied a ground-floor area of 16,000 square feet, reconstructed expressly to meet its needs. In addition to its own entrance and check room, facilities include an exhibition gallery, auditorium, art reference library, studio, snack bar and sales desk. The trend towards establishing specialized areas for young people within the larger art museums has meanwhile accelerated. They are rarely called children's museums but, in order to interest older students also, are given such names as Junior Museum, Youth Wing, or Student Center. The following are some notable examples, all from the last decade.

The Junior Gallery and Creative Arts Center in Kansas City, opened in 1960. A large portion of the museum ground floor was remodelled to provide exhibition areas, an auditorium, workshops, and studios. The following year a children's library was added.

The Junior Museum of the Art Institute of Chicago, which opened in 1964, occupies an area of 14,500 square feet, obtained by remodelling a vacated section of the ground floor. It is handsomely installed, carpeted, and air-conditioned, and includes an assembly court, exhibition gallery, foyer, auditorium, library, studio, picnic room and sales counter.

In 1964, too, the Art Center of the Museum of Modern Art obtained new quarters of its own under the elevated east end of the expanded Sculpture Garden. The area of 11,053 feet was very effectively designed for the needs of the museum's educational programme, which places the emphasis on creative art classes and research to discover, test, and demonstrate new methods of teaching. In addition to six studios with observation space, arranged around a central study and research centre, the lobby provides a comfortable waiting area and space for small exhibitions. There is a separate entrance from 54th Street as well as access by a corridor to the east wing of the museum. While the art

centre serves adults as well as children, its children's work is so extensive that it unquestionably belongs here.

The School Services of the National Museum of Anthropology occupy a handsome and well-designed area in the splendid new building opened in 1964. On the ground floor are checking facilities, a staging area, an auditorium, classrooms and a puppet theatre. The window wall gives access to a sunken patio with a small outdoor theatre. From here a stairway leads to the central patio of the museum. There is also a separate ground-floor entrance. The area is flooded with daylight and attractively furnished with tables and chairs, and facilities for creative-art activities. Up to 4,000 children a day are accommodated. The teacher guides, drawn from the schools, receive special museum training.

The Wintersteen Student Center at the Philadelphia Museum of Art was opened in 1969. It is ingeniously provided with access from the outside via a bridge entrance and from the inside via a corridor. Generous exhibition space, an attractive, automated refreshment area, a children's shop, checkroom and wash-rooms are provided. The Philadelphia museum already had well-equipped studios and an auditorium which young people continue to share with older students and adults.

A Junior Art Gallery for the Huntington Galleries in West Virginia is under construction, part of a large building addition designed by Walter Gropius. Nearing completion at the Cleveland Museum of Art is a new educational wing designed by Marcel Breuer. It will have an auditorium, a large studio, eight classrooms with sinks, a visual-aid centre, and exhibition space. Ground had been broken for a new educational wing at the Delgado Museum in New Orleans, Louisiana.

It should be pointed out that young people are never restricted to a junior museum. Their special centre within the museum is a place for them to gather, leave their coats, buy souvenirs, move and talk freely, and attend exhibitions and events planned especially for them, but they can and do also visit the museum's permanent collections and special exhibitions, which give junior museums a richness and depth that are beyond the scope of separate children's museums. The latter usually concentrate on creative workshops and exhibitions of work; some also include drama, writing, poetry, music and dance.

The impressive and continuing development of museum facilities for the young is but one facet of an upsurge of interest in the United States in all the arts which first became noticeable about 1950 and has been gaining momentum ever since. It can be seen in museum attendance statistics, in the proliferation of new museums, commercial galleries, symphony orchestras, theatrical groups, and dance companies, in the sales of books and records and art supplies. Ambitious cultural or performing arts centres have been built in cities, colleges and universities (these often include one facility for children—a museum, a library, or a puppet theatre).

Many reasons have been suggested for this 'cultural explosion'—the higher educational level of the population, greater urbanization, larger incomes, more leisure time, more travel, more and more interesting museums, and the influence of the mass media. Probably all have been contributing factors. It is notable, though, that no one has claimed that the credit specifically belongs to art education.

ART EDUCATION
IN PUBLIC SCHOOLS

It is impossible to generalize about public education in the United States. Each locality is responsible for its own policy, curriculum, staff and budget, subject only to certain broad regulations laid down by the states and by the Federal Government. It is nevertheless widely recognized that the teaching of art in our schools has always suffered almost everywhere from neglect, inadequate financial support, and a shortage of qualified teachers.

From 1900 to 1930 art in the elementary schools (ages 6–12) normally consisted of seasonal handiwork projects, such as Hallowe'en, Christmas, and Valentine decorations, the drawing of autumn leaves and spring flowers, and occasional 'picture study', consisting of sentimental and anecdotal stories about famous paintings, which each child studied with the aid of 3-inch by 4-inch black-and-white reproductions supplied for his notebook. These were taught by the regular classroom teacher, and were optional.

More progressive education in the thirties and forties, and the efforts of a handful of dedicated art educators gradually introduced a new philosophy, and new methods of teaching which aimed at allowing the child to nurture his originality and express his own ideas in a variety of materials. The emphasis was on doing; art appreciation as such was out of favour. With the increasing interest in all of the arts in recent years, however, and the rapid and widespread development of educational facilities and programmes in our art museums, there has been a renewed interest in enriching curricula by including art wherever it can be related to other subjects, in teaching the humanities—including some art history and appreciation—and even more specifically, in teaching children how to look at works of art. In many communities, these activities are being officially written into the curriculum from elementary level onwards.

In all these aspects, however, art is still normally taught by the general teacher who is often unequipped for the job. The new philosophy and new methods spread slowly, and are not yet everywhere accepted. Too many administrators still give art a very low priority in space, time, and money. Art supervisors in the school systems attempt to help teachers through workshops, in-service courses and conferences. In communities with museums like those mentioned above, the museum staff plays an active role, not only in teaching children but also by devising programmes and materials for teachers.

Carol singing at the Toledo Museum of Art —
an aspect of an extensive programme in music.
(Photo: The Blade, Toledo, Ohio.)

Floaters and Flyers: students in a sculpture
class work on all kinds of objects that float or
fly. (Photo: Junior Arts Center, Los Angeles.)

MUSEUM AND SCHOOL

Museums in the United States hardly ever have formal, official relationships with schools, covering educational policy, standards, budget, and division of responsibility. Instead, on their own initiative, they have developed programmes and found funds to support them, and then offered them free or at a nominal fee to children and to schools, believing that there is a need for such programmes and that providing them is perhaps the most appropriate public service they can render in return for their tax-exempt status.

This informal arrangement worked well in many communities for many years. In the last decade, however, the demand for museum services of all kinds has become so large as to swamp the resources of even the biggest and wealthiest institutions. Some school services have responded to appeals for help. In Cleveland, Philadelphia, and New York City, a few teachers are now assigned to work in museums to help with the school programme. In other communities, the Board of Education pays, e. g. admission or guidance fees which may be required of visiting classes. These, however, are the exception rather than the rule.

MUSEUM METHODS IN ART EDUCATION

Gallery talks

The earliest method of instruction and still the most widely practised is the gallery talk. Children come during school hours with their teacher, who has chosen a topic that can be related to the collections in the museum. Arrangements are made in advance; it is ideal if the museum can provide printed materials which help the teacher to prepare the class for the visit. The talk may directly relate to the school curriculum, but teachers increasingly tend to choose a subject because it is timely (e.g. a special exhibition) or helps to accustom the children to the museum and to looking at works of art. Gallery talks are also offered at weekends and during vacations to individual children, to children and their parents, and to groups of all kinds.

Methods vary among museums and lecturers and are influenced by the age of the children and the purpose of the visit. At their best a lively dialogue is established, with the children participating actively. Their teachers are frequently amazed to observe how well slow learners and poor readers respond when the questions can be answered by looking at real objects; and museum lecturers are often astonished to learn that an especially responsive class whose members have made acute and original observations, is 'the slowest in the school'. There is surely a lesson here for all educators.

Many museums set aside objects that can be handled during talks. For the programme *Knights in Armor*, our Junior Museum at the Metropolitan Museum of Art has a helmet and a gauntlet that can be tried on, and a piece of chain mail to be passed around; and this try-out is always the high point of the day. The Brooklyn Museum, which has rich ethnological collections, has handling material for almost all subjects.

The Philadelphia Museum of Art provides an interesting variation on the gallery talk: *Art Demonstration*, a ninety-minute programme offered, by appointment, four days a week at 10 a.m. to Grades 4–12 (ages 9–17). In a studio atmosphere, students watch an artist at work and listen to his explanations. The programme includes slides and music as background, correlated material and—time permitting—a short trip to a Museum Gallery. Five different programmes are offered each semester: *Painting a Still Life*; *Painting People*; *Experimental Drawing*; *Relief Printing*; and *Collage and Construction*.

The National Collection of Fine Arts in Washington, D. C. has developed another variation: 'improvisational tours' in which theatre techniques are used to get children to act out and thus enter into the spirit of the paintings and sculptures shown.

Depending on the ingenuity of the education staff, topics for gallery talks can be as varied as the collections and special exhibitions themselves. The purpose is not to teach facts but to awaken interest and provide enjoyment and an understanding of the rewards and pleasures a museum has to offer. Hence neither the visit nor the talk should last too long—far better that the children leave wishing for more, rather than longing for a release from walking and thinking and looking. In New York City the combination of the free-bus schedule, museum hours, and school-dismissal time suggest a stay of approximately three hours. At the Metropolitan this is broken up into a 1-hour gallery talk, a related film or studio session (15–45 minutes), a lunch period, a time for buying souvenirs, and a free period which never exceeds 45 minutes. With this much variety, 3 hours seem to pass quickly: 3 hours without variety, however, would be far too long.

In some communities the school and the museum arrange for all of the classes of a particular grade to visit the museum during the course of the year for a selected topic that fits in with school studies. Often it is Grade 6 (average age 11). Not only are children of this age particularly responsive to museum teaching but it is the last year when they are taught by a single teacher who is able to take them on trips without disturbing the school schedule. In a few places, where the museum's educational programme is extensive—and the school population not too large—almost every class visits the museum every year. At the Toledo Museum of Art, nearly 80 per cent of the city's schoolchildren are reached, and Grades 1–6 visit from six to eight times each year. Most museums, however, publish a programme showing what parts of the curriculum it concerns and suitable age levels, and then leave it to the individual teachers to make appointments for their classes; few do as well as Toledo.

Special exhibitions

Many museums for the young regard special exhibitions as an important part of their programmes. Usually the purpose is self instruction. They use simple narrative labelling and now generally include audio-visual devices to attract attention, stimulate interest, and provide graphic or dramatic explanations. Sometimes the 'labelling' is provided by taped sound. The most successful invite some active participation.

Each museum has its own exhibition policy and philosophy, influenced obviously by its own scope, the material that happens to be available, and local interests. Our Junior Museum at the Metropolitan looks for subjects not easy to handle if we rely only on the permanent collections, subjects which will awaken and broaden interests, enrich school studies, and provide a background which helps children to understand and enjoy the museum's collections, e.g. the re-creation of periods in history (*Paul Revere* [1944], *E Pluribus Unum* [1947], *The Age of Discovery—By Caravan and Caravel* [1957], *How to Look at Sculpture* [1960]); scholarship, methods and achievements (*Archaeology—Exploring the Past* [1962]).

The Artist's Workshop—Tools and Techniques: this shows the variety of techniques used in the pictorial arts from ancient to modern times: how artists make mosaics and tapestries, paint in watercolours, tempera, oil, and fresco on such varying materials as canvas, cloth, glass and clay; and how an artist's choice of medium affects his work. There are reproductions of a prehistoric cave and a Renaissance painter's studio, talking labels, peep-hole viewers, short films and slide stories. Eighty-five original works of art from the museum's collections are included, works of such quality as a Florentine altarpiece, presented by Robert Lehman, tempera panels by Simone Martini, a Dürer woodblock, and an *Adoration of the Shepherds* by El Greco. The aim is to interest children in materials and methods—to encourage them to look beyond the subject of a picture and find out all they can about how it was made, with what materials, in what kind of studio. Owing to the complexity of the subject many labels

67

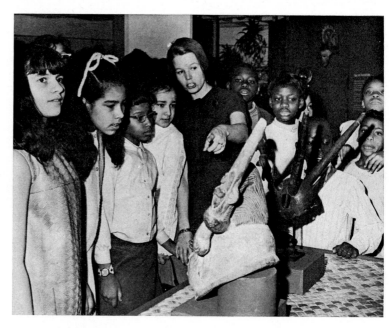

Impact Africa: exhibition at the Philadelphia
Museum of Art. (Photo: Jules Schick,
Philadelphia.)

Touring the museum. (Photo: Norton Simon,
Los Angeles County Museum of Art.)

Putting on a marionette show. (Photo: Charles Brenneke, Kansas City, Missouri.)

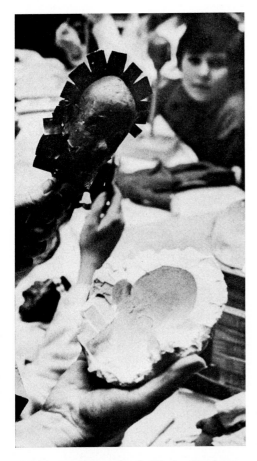

Making a marionette head. (Photo: Charles Brenneke, Kansas City, Missouri.)

were needed. For a real change of pace we are now planning to present a subject which will require almost no explanation, following what Stuart Silver, Manager of our Department of Exhibition and Design calls 'the pleasure principle'.[1]

A particularly imaginative and successful exhibition was created by Victor d'Amico and his staff at the Museum of Modern Art in New York City in 1942. Called the *Children's Art Carnival*, it has been presented annually at the museum, has been featured in United States trade fairs in Milan and Barcelona (1956), and in the United States Pavilion at the Brussels World's Fair (1958). In 1962 a replica of the carnival was set up in New Delhi, India, where it was presented by Mrs. John F. Kennedy to Mrs. Indira Ghandi as a gift of the International Council of Museums and of the Asia Society.

What is the *Children's Art Carnival*? It consists of two sections, an introductory area, and a workshop area that allows practical participation. Entrance is by way of the Contour Gate, a metal rod outline of a child of 4 and a child of 12 denoting the age range invited. Others may observe through glass panels. The introductory area, in semi-darkness, contains specially designed toys displayed in pools of light—such things as a caressable cat, a dancing rooster, a magnetic picture maker, a game table, a giant builder, and a space-ship design projector. Background music contributes to the wonderland atmosphere. As the children play freely with the toys and games, they are being introduced to colour, texture, rhythm and good design—all without words. Emerging into the brightly lit and gaily painted Studio Workshop, the children find the walls banked with adjustable easels and the centre of the room given over to two round tables with tools, and trays of enticing materials. The children

work freely for up to an hour and usually make several paintings, collages, or constructions which are theirs to take home.

Staff who have accompanied the carnival on its travels report that it works with equal success no matter where it is. There appear to be no barriers—of language, of cultural background, or lack of previous art experience.

Auditorium programmes

Museums offer a wide range of auditorium programmes for children. Educational and documentary films are very successful for several reasons. Children like them; they are readily available but seldom shown by commercial cinemas and television; they allow the museum to present information not otherwise obtainable, and to branch out in any direction—either exploring a subject in depth, or presenting a stimulating mixture; they are relatively inexpensive to rent, and require little staff time; they add variety to the programme and can serve a large audience as well as a small one.

Lectures, illustrated with slides, films, or objects, are also widely offered. The lecturer may be from the staff or outside. For eight seasons our junior museum has offered a Saturday afternoon lecture series entitled *Archaeology Around the World*. During that time, thirty-seven professional archaeologists have talked to the children and shown slides of their sites. The lecturers are paid and we charge for the series ($4 for five lectures), so that the programme is self-supporting.

Concerts: the Brooklyn Museum has a musicologist on the staff and has offered a children's concert series for the last fifteen years (including a feature on old instruments, the ancestors of those used today). It includes lecture-demonstrations on the music of various people in its programmes for schools.

Artists sometimes give demonstrations and talk about their work in the museum auditorium, but this is probably more effective in the more informal gallery or classroom demonstration where the children can come

---

1. His philosophy of museum exhibitions, with four-colour illustrations of 'The Artist's Workshop', is explained in the November 1969 issue of the British periodical *The Connoisseur*.

and go, get closer to the work, and ask more questions.

Plays and puppet shows are usually professional productions, but may be put on by children in the museum's own clubs or workshops. The Junior Gallery in Kansas City has long had successful puppet and marionette classes, and one was inaugurated last year at the Junior Art Gallery of the Huntington Galleries for a special exhibition, *A String of Puppets*.

The Metropolitan produces a quite elaborate stage presentation (with one day reserved for members and their children). An original script is prepared by a talented member of the staff, who also directs; professional actors, dancers, musicians, and entertainers as well as up to fifty volunteers are used to put the story across, with the aid of slides on multiple screens, film clips, special projection devices, costumes, scenery, dramatic lighting and sound effects. Subjects have included *The Museum Comes to Life*, *Echoes from a Castle in Spain* (for the opening of the museum's patio from Velez Blanco), *Apprentice in a Palace* (Michelangelo and the Medici) and *A Voyage to Tahiti* (on Gauguin).

Creative art classes

Probably the most common of all afterschool activities for children are creative art classes and workshops of all kinds: drawing, painting, sculpture, ceramics, mosaics, maskmaking, collage and assemblage, puppetry, print-making, batik, weaving, rug-making, photography, film-making, kite-making, liquid graphics, dance, drama, poetry, jazz—all can be found in American museums. As a rule each class is offered for a specific, rather narrow age range, sometimes beginning as low as age 3. However, a number of museums offer classes for children and parents together; these are a popular and effective way of involving parents in today's art education.

Many museums have studios especially equipped for creative work. Others use classrooms or galleries. In the summer the simpler activities are often moved outdoors, weather permitting.

Workshop teachers may be full time; more often, they are engaged part time to each one or more courses. They are as likely to be artists by profession as teachers. The museum usually charges a modest tuition fee, just enough to cover the cost of materials, or of materials and instruction.

Museums that place particular emphasis upon creative work and offer many classes (1,000–3,000 children a year) include the Museum of Modern Art, the Toledo Museum of Art, the Nelson Gallery, and the Junior Arts Center in Los Angeles. The Cleveland Museum of Art had an extensive creative art programme for many years which will be resumed when the new educational wing is completed. It has been temporarily without studio space for the past two years.

Courses

Courses for schoolchildren in art appreciation, art history, and the humanities are increasingly available. Enrolment is voluntary, as no official credits are given. The Junior Museum of the Art Institute of Chicago this year offered a fifteen-week course (on Saturdays from 1.00 to 3.30 p.m.) entitled 'Movies —the Story of a New Art'. The Cleveland Museum announced four courses for spring 1970, beginning with 'Introduction to the Museum for Children Ages 6 and 7 and their Parents'. For 7- and 8-year-olds the title was 'Viewpoints in the Galleries' in which a musician, a writer, and a dancer attempted to show how the museum's collections relate to their particular art. For youngsters of 9–12, there was 'The City in Art' and, for teenagers, 'Film Making in the Museum'.

During the summer of 1969 the Brooklyn Museum offered a Black Art Seminar; thirteen students, aged 12–16, attended the sixteen sessions wholly devoted to African, Haitian and Afro-American art.

The Junior Museum at the Metropolitan has offered a vacation course for students

Black Art Seminar at Brooklyn Museum.

Workshop, Children's Art Carnival, Brussels
World Fair. (Photo: André Monville, Ghent.)

Children's Art Carnival at Brussels World Fair.
(Photo: Sado, Brussels.)

Artist demonstrating a print technique,
Art Institute of Chicago. (Photo: Martin
J. Schmidt, Chicago.)

Trying on a helmet,
Metropolitan Museum of Art.

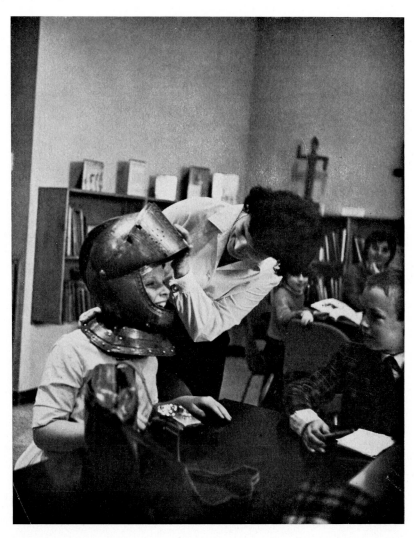

aged 12–15 each summer for the last four years. Titles were 'How to Look at Works of Art', 'History of Painting from the Renaissance to the Present', and 'Learning to Look'. A Saturday subscription course for children aged 10–14, officially entitled 'Our Museum: A Key to How It Works', but affectionately dubbed 'The Key Club', met for fifteen sessions, beginning in September 1968.

The Toledo Museum of Art is unique, I believe, in offering a five-year graded programme of music courses for children beginning with 'Adventures in Music' at age 8 and continuing through Music I, II, III and IV. In addition there is a chorus made up primarily of students in the museum's art and music classes.

Gallery games

Treasure hunts, quiz guides, paper tours and 'Find It' are some of the names given to devices, usually mimeographed, that are prepared and distributed by the staff to interest children in making repeated visits to the galleries or to special exhibitions. They involve figuring out clues which lead to specific objects, then answering questions that require careful looking. Sometimes a credit or reward is offered, but more often the activity is its own reward.

JUNIOR MEMBERSHIPS

Special events, discounts and other privileges are offered to children who hold some form of membership (i.e. children of the museum's adult members, or junior members in their own right). Usually there is an annual fee, but sometimes, as at the Brooklyn Museum, junior membership is free. The Brooklyn enrols children in Grades 1–12, provides after-school studios, Saturday and holiday recreational activities and a Junior Membership Gallery in which to exhibit work. Saturday activities in March 1970, for example, were 'Kaleidoscope', 'Stick 'Em Up' (pasting plastic straws, foam rubber, etc.), 'Sew What',

'Totem Poles', 'Signs', 'The Third Dimension', 'One-shot Shops', and 'Find It'. Older children (Grades 7–12) could choose a seminar—Survey of Modern Sculpture, Beginning Photography, or Organic Sculpture.

Century II, an eighteen-month centennial membership for children at the Metropolitan Museum of Art, provides Saturday gallery suggestions, an art book of their choice, a monthly newsletter, and five special events—one for each of the centennial exhibitions. Century II members wearing their identifying buttons also enjoy unlimited free admissions to exhibitions and discounts at the museum shops. The eighteen-month membership costs $35. Approximately half of the members are enjoying scholarships contributed by the museum's adult members and friends.

PUBLICATIONS AND SALES

Increased attendance has produced a growing market for inexpensive publications, reproductions, art materials, and other educational material for children. The publications are usually written by the educational staff or selected by them. Museums often exchange such publications. Distinguished art books for children are customarily available, though, because of the price, it is usually the parent or grandparent who buys them. Almost every junior museum has its own sales desk and even museums without junior areas often have a separate children's shop, frequently run by volunteers.

It is interesting to note how many children's book written by museum staff have been published in recent years. Authors include children's lecturers, art teachers, archaeologists and their wives, curators, museum directors—additional evidence of greater public interest—and demand!

HELPING TEACHERS

While junior museums, not surprisingly, plan for a young public, they almost all offer some programmes for teachers as well. In-service courses have the longest history. Usually held on weekdays after school, they survey the collections in whole or in part through gallery talks and slide lectures, and seek to relate museum objects to the school curriculum through discussion and individual assignments. The courses count for salary increment purposes in most school systems.

The Museum of Modern Art aims at improving creative art teaching through teacher (and parent) education. Since 1937, it has provided free art workshops for New York City elementary school-teachers. In addition a summer school, The Kearsarge Art Center, established in 1961 (when the museum purchased an old barge, *The Kearsarge*, beached at Long Island), works increasingly for teacher education. Publications, circulating exhibitions—and even a network television series—have been created by Victor D'Amico and his associates to spread an understanding of creative teaching in art. Probably most influential of all, the museum nurtured and for some twenty years sponsored an organization of art teachers and educators which grew into the National Committee on Art Education. Through its annual conferences, study sessions, research, publications, special exhibitions, and the stand it took against commercialism and against outmoded methods of all kinds, this Committee, with a peak membership of some 1,200, provided strong and progressive leadership when it was very badly needed.

In addition to courses, conferences and individual consultations with teachers, almost every museum produces materials for school use. The simplest are information leaflets, outlining the museum's educational facilities and telling the teachers how to make an appointment. Many museums produce teachers' guides or student preparation materials on their special exhibitions and on their permanent collections. These are free. Some museums rent slides, films and circulating exhibitions, and most sell publications and reproductions.

A relatively new development is the packaging of educational materials in multi-media kits. Some combination of books, pamphlets, slides, films, film-strips and objects (reproductions or originals) on a single subject are packaged together and offered for rental or, more often, for sale. In 1964, the Children's Museum in Boston, under a contract with the United States Office of Education, began to produce a prototype series of such kits called *Match Boxes*. Subjects include *Japanese Family 1966*, *A House in Ancient Greece*, and *The City*. It is hoped that the market will prove large enough to warrant commercial production and distribution.

The Metropolitan Museum's Department of Education has prepared a series of eight multi-media programmes for secondary students called *Discovering American History Through Art*. Each contains a colour filmstrip, record, colour reproductions, and a teacher's manual with background information about art and music and about the artists included. These are being produced and distributed nationally by the Rand McNally Company of Chicago, with a royalty going to the museum.

A similar arrangement with the Crowell-Macmillan Company of New York will provide national distribution for The Metropolitan Museum of Art School Exhibition Service, a programme which will 'publish' six panel exhibitions annually for subscribing schools. The schools also purchase frames into which the panels fit. Accompanying each exhibition are slides, a recorded lecture, curriculum integration manuals, posters, colour reproductions, and teaching guides.

NEW DIRECTIONS 1970

In all aspects of life in the United States there is growing pressure for innovation and change. Museum work for children is no exception. Whenever museum people get together it is the new idea, the new project, the new theory, the new development that attracts attention. Some have been described

77

Dancer in the galleries, course for 7- and 8-year olds, Cleveland Museum of Art. (Photo: Olga Rödel.)

Arranging type and printing in the exhibition
Illustrated Books for Children, Israel Museum,
Jerusalem. (Zev Radovan.)

Arranging type and printing in the exhibition
Illustrated Books for Children, Israel Museum,
Jerusalem. (Photo: Emka Ltd.)

above. However, four pervasive influences that give an impetus to many of today's innovations deserve separate mention.

There is a trend in primary and elementary education in the United States today towards providing freer, less-structured educational environments, and placing more emphasis on learning than on teaching. A wealth of carefully selected materials is provided, and children are invited to discover for themselves what the materials can do. The underlying purpose is to preserve the joy of learning which very young children exhibit so conspicuously and, at the same time, to obtain first-hand practical experiences to provide a firm foundation for future thinking. While in a sense museums, with their open collections of interesting objects, have always provided certain opportunities, the real emphasis today is on providing materials that children can manipulate and experiment with and organize in new ways. The Children's Museum in Boston has completely redesigned its former auditorium to provide such an environment, primarily for science and social studies. In art, the best example would still be the Museum of Modern Art's Children's Art Carnival, which anticipated the present movement by at least twenty years!

Another development derives from technology. Artists, exhibitions auditorium, resource centres, workshops are incorporating every imaginable kind of projection, of light and sound production, with automated devices, in every possible combination, to create new and arresting effects. If this continues museums will have to be wired like small cities and, even in art museums, prospective staff will need to study electronics, lasers and computers just for a start!

However, the most significant new direction is decentralization. Each move has been prompted by local factors, but there is a common denominator: the need and the desire to take activities to where people live, whether they be prosperous suburbs or city ghettos.

In 1957, the Detroit Institute of Arts raised private funds to finance Extension Services, a programme for suburban communities. The suburb provided space and some equipment; the museum undertook to provide staff and materials, and arrange programmes similar to those offered at the central museum—workshops for pre-school, elementary, secondary school and family groups, as well as adult lecture courses. A collection of objects, slides, and other visual materials was circulated from centre to centre. The programme began with four suburbs and, within four years, grew to sixteen.

In 1968 the same museum inaugurated Project Outreach. A three-year pilot programme, supported by the National Endowment for the Arts, the city of Detroit, and the museum's own funds, Outreach sends exhibits to communities throughout the state as well as to parks in the inner city. The exhibits are transported in an artmobile, or by station wagon in the case of the park shows, which consist of five water-proof, plexiglass cases containing three-dimensional reproductions. Outreach is directed to adults, and includes various activities for them. The exhibitions are regularly viewed by thousands of children.

In November 1967, the Whitney Museum of American Art in New York City opened an art resources centre in a converted warehouse in a poor neighbourhood on the lower East Side. The centre contains workshops for children interested in painting and sculpture as well as for professional artists who teach the children, a gallery for works of art from the Whitney, and classroom space. Three foundations and the Junior League of the City of New York contributed $60,000 to establish the centre.

The Brooklyn Children's Museum has been operating a lively and successful museum called Muse in a remodelled automobile show-room since May 1968. Its basic collections deal with science and social studies, but it occasionally shows borrowed art exhibitions, and regularly arranges workshops in poetry, painting, theatre, music and dance. It remains open until 10 p.m. from Tuesday to Friday, with evening programmes of interest to teenagers (including 'jam sessions' and jazz concerts). A lecture and workshop course for parents was held on fifteen Thursday evenings early in 1969. The subject was how to help their children to learn.

In March 1969, the Museum of Modern Art opened a Children's Art Carnival in a remodelled garage provided by the Harlem School of the Arts in New York City where it serves 780 youngsters each week. The museum has agreed to sponsor the project for three years. Plans for a mobile carnival—to be called the Caravan of Modern Art—are ready, waiting only for the funds. Each caravan would have two 40-foot trailers, and it is hoped to put several of them on the road.

The Museum of Fine Arts in Boston, with the support of a private donor and of the Massachusetts Council on the Arts and Humanities, operated a pilot mobile workshop called *Artabout* in 1969. A borrowed van visited each of seven communities for six days. Tuesdays to Fridays there were daytime workshops in sculpture and pottery for children aged 8–12. Evenings were reserved for discussions with parents and teachers, Saturdays and Sundays for general visiting by the community, with two hostesses on hand to talk about the programme and to show slides and films. A final report and evaluation has been prepared by the museum.

As one of its centennial projects, the Metropolitan Museum of Art's Department of Education is helping fourteen junior leagues (a national women's service organization) to arrange projects in their communities, each based on local interests and needs. Several are intended for schools. The members visit local schools, taking visual aids supplied by the museum and talking to individual classes. One gives a talk on archaeology, another on American paintings, another on Pre-Columbian art, yet another is helping a school to make its own 'Mini-Met Museum'. Other leagues are planning for adults. They invite

local groups for coffee and a viewing of the Metropolitan's *First Hundred Years*, and a preview of its five centennial exhibitions. Some are taking a similar programme to hospitals, to adult groups and to housing projects. One league held an exhibition in a local library, and another organized an 'Art Happening' —an all-community art show—in the school.

The Metropolitan Museum, in co-operation with the city authorities, started a mobile experiment in visual education called *Eye Opener* in July 1970. It travels about the city on a flat trailer from which an inflatable structure rises when the van stops in housing projects, big and little parks, playgrounds, streets, and vacant lots. Young and old from every neighbourhood will be invited to come to the exhibition, which is designed to encourage visitors to become better observers. The first *Eye Opener* exhibition is called *The Spiral Show*. It is built around the spiral forms that are common in nature, everyday objects, and works of art, and ranges from shells, horns, pine cones and springs to old jewellery from the Near East and Chinese damasks. There will be a 4-minute film of spiral motions, a fingerprint wall, a 24-inch Kalliroscope made by Paul Matisse (grandson of the painter), and a continuous slide show of paintings and other art objects which cannot travel with the exhibition.

A trustee committee is making a study of other ways in which the museum can extend its resources and services out into the community, and particularly into areas of the city where there is now very little cultural opportunity.

Not all of the mobile projects are as elaborate as those just mentioned. The Hudson River Museum in Yonkers, New York, last summer simply sent staff out to the parks and playgrounds with push carts full of art materials!

Finally, innovation is prompted by the financial squeeze on most museums in recent years. Desperately needing new sources of income, many museums have boldly and imaginatively developed programmes that are self-supporting or even income-producing. In the competition for grants, too, they have learned that new ideas succeed. Behind decentralization is the belief that tomorrow's supporters—and voters—must be reached today.

An ever-growing attendance, the pressure for change, and serious financial problems represent a major challenge. I believe we are on our way to meet it and that, in retrospect, it will prove to have been beneficial. Already our museums are livelier, more interesting, and more responsive than they have ever been.

John Read

Television and the museum 6

I was doing some research for a television film about Albrecht Dürer in the Albertina in Vienna. A young American teacher came into the room and requested to see the famous drawing by Dürer, *Hands of an Apostle*. Obviously she must have seen reproductions of this work many times before, but now the original was carefully brought and placed on a stand before her. She was lost in contemplation of it for ten minutes. It was an experience for her that television cannot emulate. Ten minutes! That same drawing will be seen in the film for perhaps only ten seconds. Yet I do not believe that television is of necessity superficial. I know that whereas a visit to a museum may not induce one to watch television, the reverse process is certainly common. The American teacher's ten-minute communion with Dürer may well have been prompted by a programme that she once saw.

Who sees these television programmes that feed themselves on the possessions of the world's museums? Millions of people, and certainly more people than ever find their way into a museum. We are active communicators in a mass medium. We may debate how large a minimum-sized audience can be, but there has never been any debate about our need to communicate to our audiences, large or small. If we fail, our audience has gone and the programme might as well not exist. In general, mass communication is a

new experience for museum and gallery staff. They have got used to their 'private views' and press days. They are familiar with the requirements of publishers, and write and publish books themselves. They have even understood the need to publish postcards, but there, sometimes, the matter ends. But of course museums are becoming increasingly involved in public as well as private patronage, and when this happens some of them see new opportunities in their changed role in society. They become a part of a system of leisure, arts and education. Their collections are used as well as conserved. There is a new demand for a new kind of knowledge from a new public. This public is familiar with the techniques of television and often expects more of an exhibition than the museum has ever imagined trying to give. The concept of 'a museum without walls' originated, I believe, in the mind of André Malraux. It would seem a little difficult for any architect to achieve a literal embodiment of this idea, but perhaps television can claim to have developed the thought by bringing the possessions of museums into the daily viewing experience of millions of families in their homes.

From the museum's point of view is this at best a nuisance, and at its worst a menace? Or is it something to be welcomed as an extension of the museum's legitimate activity?

It depends on how one defines a museum's role in society. Should it be a mine of information or simply a safe deposit? Should it play an active role in presenting and inter-

John Read is Senior Producer, BBC Television, London.

preting its collection, or is it purely a centre for study, conservation and research? After all, a few museums are already directly in the television business themselves. They have their cameras, their lights and their studios. They have recording apparatus on which to store their programmes, and projection apparatus on which to show them. They interview artists and visiting celebrities. They record temporary exhibitions. They prepare lectures by their staff and they make studies of living artists who work in their region. They even tour their programmes around halls and schools outside the museum in a mobile van that brings the museum to the people. Last year at the Grand Palais in Paris, Marc Chagall made a visit to his retrospective exhibition, and in the lecture hall he answered questions for an hour from schoolchildren who had come to meet him. The museum staff televised all this while it was happening, with their apparatus, and showed it repeatedly throughout the exhibition halls and foyers for many weeks.

It seems but a small step to take for the museums to enter directly into full-scale television production and distribution, just as they have often already entered into the world of publishing. After all, people will soon be buying television cassettes to play on their receivers at home, just as they buy records now. But it is one thing to stand up and give a slide lecture to thirty dedicated people. It is quite another thing to write a book that will sell. It is even more complicated to make a television programme that the general public will watch. I think it is unlikely that the museums will want to take over the production of programmes on existing public television channels, but I do think it is time for museums to recognize the existence of television, to understand its needs and problems, and to consider its potential for their own development. For this reason it is worth attempting to define the evolution of television arts programmes, for it is these that bear most directly on the museums' activities. It has become a far more

sophisticated business than simply sending the cameras down to the gallery just because the director thinks that by 'appearing on the box' he is going to do himself and his museum a little bit of good. We have tried that, and usually it doesn't work.

In the early days of television 'immediacy' was the magic quality we all sought. Television, it was argued, was the process of seeing things happen as they happen. For some reason, a film passing through a projector was not a happening. The film camera was in disrepute, and the fashion was to play with the electronic giants that transmitted pictures 'live' into people's homes. In our excitement about the 'life' of the picture, we rather forgot that our audience was alive as well and perfectly capable of switching off when they got bored. The constraining walls of the cinema, the theatre and the museum had indeed vanished and so had the compulsion to stay in one's seat for fear of being seen to walk out. Of course in those days television visited museums and art galleries in the same happy pioneering spirit that took us into theatres, circuses, ballrooms, swimming pools and religious services. 'It was happening now, wasn't it?'—so it was television.

In the course of time television programming matured. We came to rely less on existing events that we could visit. We felt the need to make our own events and to devise our own kinds of performance. The spell of 'live' television began to wear off and people engaged in making programmes or in planning their transmission began to see advantages in using film, or recording images on tape, so that more thoughtful and effective means of communication could be devised. In that process we went through a stage of bringing museums and museum people into the television study. We assembled panels of experts and lines of objects and tried various ways of entertaining and instructing people by mixing the two together. Then as film became more respectable, we began to send the experts abroad actually to stand in the very places where the objects were and on the very ground where our cultural heritage had come into being. At the same time we began to evolve on film various kinds of cultural documentary that dealt with the work of living artists, art history and art appreciation.

Where have we got to now? In the United Kingdom, BBC Television produces and transmits 250 arts programmes every year. We endeavour, wherever the financial and legal possibilities exist, to sell as many of these as possible all over the world. We join forces with other television organizations in order jointly to produce and screen programmes that would not otherwise be an economic proposition. We have even attempted to embrace all civilization in a single series of thirteen 50-minute films written and presented by Sir Kenneth Clark, a former Director of our National Gallery, and a world authority who gave two years of his life to a project that cost us £250,000 to make. Was *Civilization—A Personal View* a museum without walls? Certainly museums all over the world contributed to it, but what made the greatest impression were those sequences filmed outside museums, in the cathedrals, churches, cities, landscapes and buildings where the physical presence of great art in its own setting gave the viewer an experience rarely contrived in a gallery or a show-case.

We have, from time to time, made films about museums themselves. The Tate Gallery, the National Gallery and the Wallace Collection, have all been treated in this manner and we are now in the process of making a film about the British Museum. This is a special problem for us, as well as the museums concerned, for in fact there is no reason at all to suppose that a museum offers a ready-made programme. A collection is not a script, and a catalogue is not usually any more interesting to read than a telephone directory. Some kind of theme or argument has to be found. Dramatic values have to be established. The history of the Tate Gallery and its functions in the present were a background to an argument, based on the collection, about the nature of taste and the re-

lation of taste to inspiration and creativity. Our heroes were the great artists, all of whom defined the commonly accepted tastes of their time. The National Gallery film relied more on showing what went on behind the scenes—restoration, conservation, security, purchase and selection—and this was the link that held together a representative selection of the gallery's treasures.

Then we have the television magazine, that is to say the regular programme that is shown once a week or once a month, on the same channel, at the same time, and catering for a particular, specialized interest. This is television reporting, relying on topicality and news value for its appeal, and we have had long experience of this kind of programme which represents a large part of our total arts programming. It began, some years ago, with *Monitor* and is now continued by *Review*. We find that in a competitive situation where the public always has the choice of three channels to watch, *Review* has a fairly stable audience in the United Kingdom of 500,000 people. This is not a sensational figure, but it compares very well with the sales of art publications and the attendances at major exhibitions which rarely go beyond 50,000 or 60,000. *Review* attempts to survey artistic developments and events in the United Kingdom and abroad and pays special attention to what is happening outside London.

We find that though most museums and galleries are quite prepared to give facilities and provide services, few are equipped to do so with the speed a topical programme requires. It takes a long time to plan a television programme, and at least some time to film, process, edit and narrate the material we get. As all BBC programmes are now made in colour we have special problems securing high-quality colour transparencies, which are often the life-blood of a story. Nor can one do very much in a gallery during the three or four hours usually given to the press for their work of photographing and reviewing. It is one thing to print a single photograph and

Animal, Vegetable, Mineral: a BBC panel
programme in which a panel of experts is
challenged to identify a series of unusual objects
selected by a museum. The exhibit in the
picture is a 35,000-year old skull of a rhino-
ceros, found in England. (Photo: BBC.)

A talk about Watteau's painting *L'Enseigne de
Gersaint* in a BBC series of programmes on art.
(Photo: BBC.)

A Fortune in Pictures: a programme explaining
how the British National Gallery works.
Cameraman filming two paintings by Veronese.
(Photo: BBC.)

An early programme in which the owners and
treasures of 'stately homes' were brought to the
studio for a live transmission programme.
(Photo: BBC.)

write 300 words. It is quite another to light and shoot an exhibition so as to have enough shots to make a 10-minute film story.

The kind of work we do will continue to suffer frustrations and limitations until it is possible for museums to send out their advance information many weeks in advance. In doing this, their publicity department should be as well informed as to who does what in television as they are in the case of the press and publishers. A single hand-out, that arrives three days before the event, simply addressed to 'The BBC' will obviously get no one anywhere. It would help also if museums automatically ensured that they held rights in their exhibits to permit us to televise them without having to make further reference to artists or owners who may not reply, or who live abroad or have gone away from their known address. Even more, it would help, if in planning the installation of their exhibitions, museums were able to amend the timing of their operation to allow television two or three days' exclusive use of the galleries for their cameras, lights and sound, before the exhibition is opened. Often we will prefer to write our own scripts and make our own choice of speakers or narrators. Ideally, planning for a really effective presentation of an exhibition on television means bringing television in from the start. The 500th anniversary exhibition of the work of Albrecht Dürer took place in Nuremberg in May 1971. I had already been working on the film for a year.

There are of course virtues in simplicity when the right formulae can be found. One of the most successful series of arts programmes that we do is also one of the cheapest. It is called *Canvas* and has been in production for several years. Originally it was a programme produced in the television studio, using the techniques of 'live' production with electronic cameras, but recording the results on tape in order to give the programme a better finish and to relieve the speakers of some of the strain of actual live transmission. The purpose was to select experts on their subject and ask them to give a detailed talk about a single painting. This painting was shown, by means of photographic blow-ups on back projection, in its original size and the programme was presented so as to establish the scale of the work in relation to the speaker, as well as providing the usual detailed study of close-ups and other related works. It was in fact the equivalent of a gallery lecture, but it took a great deal of skilful presentation to make it work.

When the studios were re-equipped for colour, it proved to be impossible to enlarge photographs to a sufficient size without a serious loss in quality. The programme was therefore re-designed and went on to film. The film cameras were sent to the galleries where the original works were to be found, and the speakers travelled with them. As a matter of policy, a number of lesser-known museums out of London were included, and amongst the speakers we selected many people, known to the public, but not authorities on art. It became a programme that reflected the non-expert's personal interests and tastes in individual works of art and was none the less instructive and illuminating for that.

The types of programme that I have been describing are all designed for the general public. I now would like to outline briefly what is done for specialized audiences, first by the television channels in the United Kingdom, and then by educational authorities.

A whole range of special programmes, some of which include the arts, are being prepared for the new Open University project, which has sometimes been referred to as 'The University of the Air'. At certain times of the day one of the BBC channels will be used to transmit programmes that supplement or amplify correspondence courses, tutorials and seminars, specially designed for students who enrol for a series of courses that will culminate in the award of a degree carrying full academic status. The students will be of any age and without the usual university entrance qualifications, though a certain educational standard is required. Then we produce another series of educational programmes which fit into voluntary adult education activities carried out by various authorities and colleges in the evenings. To this one must add the work of an entire department who make programmes in collaboration with educational advisory boards, which are shown to children at school as part of their classroom teaching. Our commercial-television networks have similar responsibilities. Finally, in London, the Greater London Educational Authority has trained teachers and provided equipment and studios so that the London State schools can make their own programmes, which are shown in the classroom on closed-circuit television. All this can be compared with similar activities in other countries. American universities have been involved for many years in the running of educational television stations and the making of programmes, and they are advised and provided with further programmes by the National Education Television Center in New York. In the Federal Republic of Germany, eighty hours a year of 'study programmes' are transmitted on the nation's third channel.

We would seem to be in the midst of a cultural or educational revolution, in which television is playing a leading part. The ultimate aims and achievements may seem to be relatively obscure, but one consequence that is already apparent is the impact this is having on services required from museums all over the world. I would certainly not like to underestimate the debt we owe to harassed museum officials who suddenly find themselves involved in our activities, about which they often know little, and for which they get little credit. My own film about the Tate Gallery would have been impossible to make without the whole-hearted support of almost every member of that institution's staff. The gallery was invaded, night and day for two weeks by a team of up to eight people. It meant special security arrangements. Staff

had to be found to supervise our activities. Overtime schedules had to be arranged. Cables and lights had to be installed in every conceivable position. We sometimes needed to exclude the public while we were working. Often we worked in galleries with the public present and being filmed themselves. Exhibits had to be moved. Fragile and quite priceless works of art were taken out of their restrictive show-cases. Trustees had to be informed and soothed. Heads of departments were consulted and nagged. The library was placed at our disposal and the gallery photographer was given nightmares preparing colour transparencies for our needs. The entire restoration department was involved in a day's shooting, and the Director of the Tate, firmly pinned behind someone else's desk, was gently persuaded to lift a few veils from the secrecy that usually surrounds a museum's affairs. The paper work was formidable. Owners had to be traced, copyright clearances obtained.

I am not surprised if sometimes television's welcome is a little cool at the gallery door. I hope that someone sometimes thinks of our problems too. The cheapest television programme about the arts may cost several thousands of pounds. The big ones may easily go to £25,000 or £30,000. But if I were asked to single out one problem that may restrict our programming more than any other, I would say that it is the fees some museums charge for the right to reproduce their work on television. Just as I feel it is absolutely essential for us to take seriously the worries many people have about the risk of damage to works of art, particularly under intensive light, so I would hope that our own economic dilemma might receive sympathetic treatment. No one has ever made a fortune out of cultural television programmes. Most of us are civil servants working for non-profit-making organizations. What we do appeals to a relatively small sector of the public. I hope that what we do is a cultural service to the public. Because television is new, museums have often not got rules and regulations that have been designed with our needs in mind. As often as not someone has to interpret a directive originally framed to apply to the press, to publishers or to advertisers.

As I have said before, a single shot in a television programme may only be on the screen for 10 seconds or less. A 50-minute film may include as many as 200 or more separate works of art. That can mean that we have to use 200 Ektachromes for which we are charged heavily. Sometimes a museum will loan their own for a nominal sum. Sometimes we bear the cost of having them made. But on top of this there is a growing custom of charging a reproduction fee of dubious legal standing for works that are not even in copyright. No one can reasonably object to some modest payment that helps to defray the cost of answering television's requests. Unfortunately there are some museums which seem to think that television is a rich source of financial patronage. Reproduction fees are inextricably included in transparency hire charges, and still have to be paid if the picture is eventually edited out of the completed programme. Others, having charged us the full commercial rate for making a

transparency, or permitted us to employ a photographer at the same rate, then insist on a reproduction fee out of all proportion to any rational assessment. If it is going to cost us £40 to be able to show a single painting for 10 seconds or less (of course what is actually shown is the photographic image, not the original), and then the museum insists that we return the transparencies which we have paid a photographer to make, so that they may be hired back to us again on some other occasion, or rented out to some other user, I fear that television arts programmes are going to be costed out of the market altogether by a small minority of rapacious individuals whose success so far may well encourage others. I think people would welcome some agreed international scale of charges and a common procedure that would ensure that a single payment allowed the television organization full rights to repeat its programmes and arrange their showing in other countries. As it is, we are approaching the stage when it would be cheaper to ask an artist to make a painting for us than to use a colour transparency of an existing work. Unfortunately there are not many people painting now called Rembrandt.

Ulla Keding Olofsson

Temporary and travelling exhibitions

7

A number of exhibitions were staged in Sweden in connexion with European Conservation Year 1970. In Stockholm, three were arranged—by the Museum of Natural History (*Survival*), by the Museum of Technology (*Man on Earth*) and the Museum of National Antiquities (*What is Cultural Environment?*, which subsequently went on tour throughout the country). Riksutställningar, Swedish Travelling Exhibitions (STE), together with the Central Office of National Antiquities and the Museum of Natural History, produced *A Country to Live in*, three identical editions of which were sent to museums where they were supplemented by exhibitions covering local conservation problems. Three hundred copies of a small nature-conservation exhibition were offered for sale to interested institutions and groups.

This way of publicizing nature conservation and the care of monuments represented a new use of the exhibition as a medium for joint planning by museums and a certain pooling of resources.

Museums are responding to the demands created by more leisure and education by producing a wider range of exhibitions—which increase attendance figures but put a strain on resources (personnel, premises and money).

There is indeed cause for concern. The *Belmont Report*, published in 1969 by the American Association of Museums, reflects a trend experienced in many countries:

Ulla Keding Olofsson works with Swedish Travelling Exhibitions, Stockholm.

The increase has been so rapid, and has reached such a level, that museums now have to turn down requests for service. Yet the times call for a sharp increase in the educational and cultural opportunities which museums are uniquely equipped to provide.

The increased demands on museums come from all ages and segments of the population, affect not only the institutions in metropolitan centres but those elsewhere, and reflect the dependence on museums of both the disadvantaged and the affluent.

So far as can be foreseen, the factors responsible for the increased demands on museums are likely to continue to prevail indefinitely.

This preliminary warning is followed by a consideration of the practical consequences in terms of finance, premises, training and —what is particularly interesting here—research, travelling exhibitions and the mass media.

In Sweden a government committee (known as MUS 65) was set up in 1965 to investigate these problems, and STE was established to investigate the role of the exhibition in contemporary society, its ability to interest people from all walks of life, reach people outside the cities, and contribute significantly to the work of schools and adult education.

The experiments with travelling exhibitions have been made in co-operation with museums, cultural agencies, education authorities, adult education services, government and regional bodies, and groups of artists, with a view to answering such questions as:

What co-ordinating role should STE play in the organization of exhibitions in Sweden? What services can it offer museums and different administrative bodies? How far should decentralization go? Should exhibition services and resources be located in different parts of the country? How should the exhibitions themselves be allocated? Who should take care of the exhibition when it reaches its destination?

A studio and workshop were acquired in 1967. In 1970 STE had a staff of about fifty, a budget of 4 million Swedish kroner ($770,000), and distributed 160 exhibitions, large and small, apart from those manufactured on a commercial basis by the hundred.

Sociological surveys were regularly made, of visitors, and of the effects of exhibitions. Sample interviews in the northern Swedish town of Gävle provided comparative data for a normal population, its cultural habits, and so on.

The results serve in subsequent planning. Thus one of the first surveys (covering a large traditional art exhibition *A Hundred Years of the National Museum*) showed that a larger proportion of new visitors came from places where outside activities were liveliest. Contact is now made with the local organizers from the very beginning so as to give them plenty of time to build up programmes relating to the theme of any proposed exhibition.

The influence of an exhibition on knowledge and attitudes has been studied in connexion with *The Camera* and other exhibitions. When television was used in conjunction with an exhibition, it was found that the group who were shown the television programme before they saw the exhibition learned most from it.

A good deal of attention has been devoted to the possibilities of various kinds of audio-visual media as supplements, or even alternatives to exhibitions. Slides and tapes have long been a staple item, but STE has also experimented with multi-picture arrangements, using electronically controlled batteries of projectors and tape recorders. Exhibition packages for schools generally include short films or film-strips to illustrate such phenomena as, for example, volcanic eruptions or earthquakes, or unique exhibits such as votive figures from classical Greece.

The early surveys provided no clear-cut conclusions. Advertisements tended to have a relatively greater influence on women, students, graduates and elderly persons. Newspaper articles tended to have more effect: the older people were, the less formal education they had had, the greater was the interest aroused. Posters had more effect on the young, on those who had had a longer formal education, and those who had no basic interest in the subject. The surveys have continued. As exhibitions have come to centre more on groups of objectives, they provide new sources of information: the motives for visits and factors influencing them; what visitors do at exhibitions; attitudes to exhibitions; capacity of the exhibition, over the longer term, to activate and stimulate.

The survey results will comprise a major part of the report to MUS 65 which will contain proposals for consideration by Parliament regarding the future organization of travelling exhibitions in Sweden, and a report on experimental activities since 1965.

In Sweden, as in so many other parts of the world, museums have endeavoured to meet the increased demands made on them—not least by schools—by producing more exhibitions (generally from ten to twenty annually). Temporary exhibitions have become a major item in every museum. And attendance figures have soared.

But the demand for the museums' services had outstripped their resources. More and more school classes were being shepherded through by overworked regular staff or casually engaged students. Only very few museums had responded by trying to make their exhibitions more informative, educational and self-explanatory and, consequently, more independent of hand-outs and experienced or inexperienced guides.

There had been a steep rise in the demand for new teaching aids. At the same time, there were large and under-exploited resources—artefacts, pictures and documents —in our museums, resources which could be made available on a completely different scale and in a completely different way from previously.

This was the origin of the STE project *The Exhibition as an Aid to Teaching*, intended to make exhibitions as natural a feature in the classroom as books, tape recorders and projectors. The exhibitions it had already produced were largely a continuation of the activities of the Society for Art in Schools (mainly screen exhibitions to be set up in corridors or other large spaces).

The new project required an exhibition small enough for the classroom; light and portable; adapted to fit in with the current school plans and syllabus (the Board of Education suggested a joint project with an experimental school in Brännan, in the north of Sweden); and easily reproducible. Consequently, prototypes were made to be tried out at Brännan, revised and then produced in batches of twenty-five—one for each county —and in still larger numbers according to demand.

The time available for the project did not allow the thorough, long-term experimentation customary in the production of teaching aids. The main concern was to show what a particular kind of teaching material would have to offer if reasonable resources were applied to its development; and to test its possibilities as a complement to the teaching activities of the museums that would make for a more efficient use of their resources while at the same time widening the scope of their activities. Moreover, the material had to be ready for the new 1970 syllabus which had already been followed for several years at Brännan. This syllabus offered radical new possibilities as regards both teaching methods and time-tables; it allowed various groups to be catered for: individual pupils, groups, combined classes; flexible class periods; and it placed a heavy emphasis on pupil participation.

Very few Swedish schoolchildren ever have the chance to see genuine exhibits from ancient Greece and Rome. The only sizeable collections are at the Mediterranean Museum in Stockholm which, from the beginning of the project, was a very interested partner in a bid to devise means of presenting its collections to a wider public. One of the first results of this collaboration was the film *Gifts to the Gods*—ancient religious beliefs as expressed in different kinds of votive offerings. This 16-mm film is in colour and runs for six minutes. It is supplemented by china replicas, commissioned by STE in consultation with the Mediterranean Museum. Examples of modern votive offerings are also included to bring the story down to our own times.

Both STE and the museum wanted material capable of redressing a certain over-concentration on the history of art in the study of ancient history in schools at present. Emphasis was therefore laid on cultural history in general; and the large and less frequently utilized collections at the museum were drawn on to recreate daily life in the ancient world. The first exhibition, *The Kitchen in Ancient Times*, consists of china replicas of ancient cooking utensils, pictures, an explanatory pamphlet, and a number of recipes which pupils can try out for themselves.

Another type of material, sadly neglected in schools, is often concealed in museum archives—letters, documents, brochures, photographs. A start has been made on publishing such material in facsimile by Jonathan Cape in England (*Jackdaws*) and Delpire in France (*Documents*). Facsimile material of this kind is of greater educational value than the printed collections generally in use if we accept the aim, implicit in modern history teaching, of enabling pupils to study source material, and do elementary research on their own.

In as small a linguistic area as Sweden, no

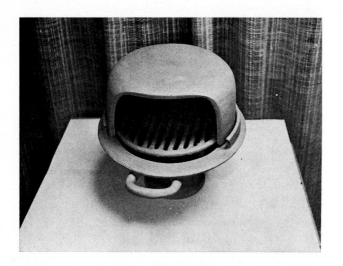

Ancient mobile oven: china replica of the original in the Mediterranean Museum, Stockholm. Included with household utensils in the exhibition package *The Kitchen in Ancient Times,* with pictures and text describing the culinary habits of the ancient world. (Photo: Riksutställningar.)

Ancient domestic utensils (mobile grill, beaker and oil lamp): china replicas of the originals in the Mediterranean Museum, Stockholm. Included with other household utensils in the exhibition package *The Kitchen in Ancient Times,* with pictures and text describing the culinary habits of the ancient world. (Photo: Riksutställningar.)

A red exhibition box asks: 'What are handicrafts?' Provides a theoretical background for study by handicraft groups. The members assemble round the screens, materials and collapsible cardboard models of domestic interiors and discuss what exactly they are doing. (Photo: Riksutställningar.)

A trunk dealing with the emigration period, *To the Land in the West*. Facsimile documents and brochures, pictures, literature, tapes for group studies culminate in an exhibition arranged by the pupils themselves. (Photo: Riksutställningar.)

An Object Reflects a World. Everyday articles such as a simple paraffin lamp or baskets made of different materials and pictures of people and places, can be made into simple dioramas. Literature for teachers and pupils. Classroom package on Tanzania for junior schools, designed to make the subject come alive and excite the pupils' curiosity. (Photo: Riksutställningar.)

Form Games: photographs mounted on cubes in the form of Chinese boxes, with an attractive surprise toy in the middle. A basis for discussions of everyday situations in nursery school, junior schools, and schools for handicapped children. (Photo: Riksutställningar.)

Environment for the Million, a small exhibition to introduce debates during European Conservation Year 1970. Concludes with the question: 'Shouldn't the individual be allowed a bit more say in the matter? What do you think?' Collapsible cardboard exhibition, 300 copies produced for sale. (Photo: Riksutställningar.)

Working-class Memories: a photographic exhibition compiled by the Nordic Museum, Stockholm, parallel to the documentary series the museum has been publishing for several years. Example of exhibition redesigned and provided with study material from Swedish Travelling Exhibitions for distribution throughout the country. (Photo: Riksutställningar.)

Our Culture in Textbooks and Real Life:
a different way of teaching the art history of the
period 1910–20. The actual exhibition room
contrasts the study of an art historian with
scenes from Swedish working life; the outsides
of the walls illustrate folk culture and its
disintegration. (Photo: Riksutställningar.)

publisher has ventured to go in for this kind of material, but STE was interested in testing a Swedish compilation (foreign material is already being used in a number of Swedish schools): Swedish emigration to America during the late nineteenth century, a period represented in the collections of practically every local museum in the country. Facsimiles can provide an introduction to further studies in the local museums.

This collection (*To the Land in the West*) comprises emigrant recruitment brochures, land prospectuses, broadsheets warning of the evils of emigration, crash courses in English for emigrants, letters, folk-songs from the period, boat tickets and instalment contracts. The aim is to give every pupil in a group material to keep, to induce him to fill in the forms, study the texts, feel the immediacy of the experience, going on perhaps to delve into the American letters in the attic at home, and finally to come up with his own views.

To the Land in the West forms part of a larger school exhibition with the same title, contained in the 'America trunk'. This includes large mounted pictures (which can be stood on tables with the aid of blocks), tapes with samples of Swedish-American dialects taken from a dialect archive, catalogues from emigration exhibitions at various museums, and statistical tables and maps for use with an epidiascope. The trunk was used by the Board of Education in the film shown to all Swedish teachers prior to the introduction of the new 1970 syllabus as an example of a new kind of study material.

The project also comprises 'country exhibitions', to meet the rising demand for material on countries outside Europe, and especially the developing countries—typical items of clothing, everyday objects, records and so on. The idea derives partially from the Ethnographical Museum in Leiden, where schoolchildren cannot only study the culture of foreign countries but dress up in their clothes, play their musical instruments, cook and eat their food, and put on simple plays.

The National Travelling Theatre (the counterpart of STE in the theatre world) now established at Brännan, has made it possible to follow the Leiden example of using museum exhibits for drama purposes.

Another variation, primarily intended for comprehensive school pupils of 14–16, is the *An Object Reflects a World* series which is being jointly compiled with the Malmö College of Education under the Unesco Associated Schools Project in Education for International Understanding and Peace.

The first country exhibition deals with Tanzania. Colour illustrations are used to present the people and their surroundings. It comprises thirty or so postcard-size pictures (encased in plastic so that they can stand up to a fair amount of punishment), and eight larger folding illustrations which make a background to plants, animals or vehicles made by the pupils or brought to school by them, the whole giving the effect of a simple diorama. This leaves more scope for the pupils' own comments and activities than ordinary slide shows.

Simple everyday objects (a rudimentary paraffin lamp, baskets made of different materials, a musical instrument) can provide the background to a discussion by pupils and teacher of such problems as development, the production of energy, the water supply, the right of a people to retain its individuality. A calendar has flaps that open to reveal pictures. Finally, there is a picture-book. This is at present available only in a limited, hand-drawn edition. A group of young artists have used drawings and photographs to make a strip cartoon which, in simplified form, summarizes complex problems such as education, help to self-help, employment, urbanization, ecology, human rights.

This project was developed jointly with a teacher-training college, and particular importance was attached to the compilation of a teacher's manual. One of the central problems in establishing the exhibition as an educational instrument is to devise instructions or methods for incorporating exhibitions in teaching. Although teachers can usually draw on their own experiences as visitors to art exhibitions, a carefully thought out method is clearly needed.

Apart from exhibitions of original works of art, a large proportion of the school exhibitions produced by STE for the Society for Art in Schools (comprising some 300 schools and education authorities throughout the country) are concerned with art education. Thus *Pictures Everywhere* (one copy to every member of the society) provides a basis for discussing pictorial communication. It is printed on sixteen pairs of cardboard screens. A separate edition has been prepared for sale to other schools and museums.

For nursery schools, junior schools and schools for handicapped children, *Form Games* includes photographs of everyday situations mounted on five cubes in the form of Chinese boxes, with an attractive surprise toy in the middle. Experimental versions have been made of plastic, masonite and cardboard. The teacher's manual deals with pictures in general and specific teaching suggestions for the material in question.

One of the first and largest STE exhibitions, *Discovery and Experience*, raised some of the major questions of aesthetic education in school. It was shown at museums in Sweden for two years, and served to establish the 'activity room' in exhibitions, since every museum receiving it had to set aside a space where teachers and pupils, parents and children and any other visitors could use various kinds of material—generally waste materials from local industries—for personal self-expression. In spite of the formidable practical difficulties at many museums, the activity room was a great success (not least with press photographers), and several schools have suggested that they be made a permanent feature of exhibitions.

In recent years STE has participated in many summer courses for teachers, either sending one of the staff along with an exhibition or providing information about the local experiments which may soon develop into a nation-wide service for schools.

In the summer of 1970 it produced its first special exhibition for a teachers' course, *Our Culture—in Textbooks and Real Life*, designed to present an alternative method of teaching the history of art and music between 1910 and 1920 in secondary schools. Participants had to plan lessons based on the exhibition, which took the form of a room containing furniture from the Nordic Museum and paintings from the National Museum showing an art historian's study, 1910–20, and large photographs on two of the walls depicting scenes from Swedish working life. The outer walls dealt with popular culture, its disintegration, the new urban culture, media, survivals and 'the optional society'. This exhibition will be shown at museums round the country, where curators can add local material, and co-operate with regional education authorities in arranging study days for teachers.

Exhibitions need not be confined, of course, to the compulsory school system. Popular education movements have long been a major sector of the educational system in Sweden, and small exhibitions produced for schools have often proved useful to them. The 'American trunk', for example, was a great success with study circles for pensioners.

Exhibitions are also specifically designed for adult education schemes, e.g. the exhibition jointly produced with ABF (the workers' educational association) and the National Concert Tour Scheme to provide a basis for discussion in music circles. Entitled *The People's Music*, it illustrates the role of folk music in Sweden, and calls for a more popular music culture. It is technically interesting in combining the impact of the large exhibition with the easy handling of the small exhibition—an important consideration, as the study circles will themselves be distributing and assembling it. The basic module is an ordinary Swedish fish box which is built up into a three-tier semi-circle. A few more fish

We Call them Developing Countries, a wide-ranging adult education project presented the State experimental scheme for the use of radio and television in education. The radio and television programmes are supplemented by an STE exhibition in the form of four screens showing objects from the countries dealt with. Here we see a hoe from Zambia, backed by the screen dealing with agricultural problems. Produced in 300 copies for sale. (Photo: Riksutställningar.)

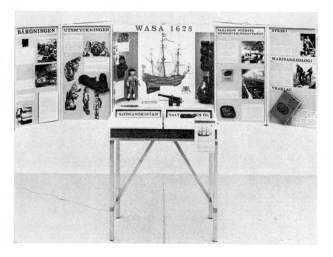

A 'red cabinet': a standard cabinet made by STE to serve as container and show-case and provided with built-in lighting. Used for example by the Wasa Museum to illustrate the salvaging and restoration of the flagship *Wasa.* Shown at libraries, cafés and camping sites in northern Sweden. (Photo: Riksutställningar.)

The People's Music: an exhibition calling for a
more popular music culture. The basic module
is an ordinary Swedish fishbox, built up into a
three-tier semi-circle. (Photo: Riksutställningar.)

boxes, covered in canvas, go to make up seats where people can listen to a large selection of music from a tape recorder built into one of the boxes.

Handicrafts are a prominent feature of the adult-education movement. The STE package exhibition *What are Handicrafts?* enables members of handicraft groups, in addition to their practical work, to discuss handicraft history and its relation to other forms of art and to social developments in general. Table-size picture screens encased in plastic, and material samples, are used to point such questions as: 'Is this homecraft, handicraft or an industrial product?' Typical domestic interiors—from the old rural society, and the middle and working classes—are illustrated by collapsible cardboard models (an idea taken from children's books). These study packages, like those included in *The Exhibition as an Educational Instrument*, are regarded as prototypes to be tested, revised and then reproduced in bulk, either in the same form or, for example, as printed cardboard screens (a medium which STE is using to reach large numbers of people in minimum time). An edition of several hundred justifies the production of explanatory books, catalogues, and audio-visual material.

Immigrants in Sweden was designed to dispel some of the ignorance which can have disastrous consequences in a country with a high rate of immigration. This exhibition (400 printed), was supplemented by a collection of essays sold at a subsidized price, and a short catalogue, available free of charge in Swedish and the main immigrant languages (Finnish, German, Italian, Greek, Serbo-Croat).

An exhibition entitled *Education or Else*, based on material on the literacy campaign compiled by the Swedish International Development Authority and the Swedish National Commission for Unesco, was printed in an edition of 200, in the form of four square pillars.

In conjunction with the Adult Education Association and the Board of Education, STE has started a pilot scheme to investigate the possibilities of adapting exhibitions in popular education to attract new categories of learners, and of devising study forms which will enable groups of different kinds to make use of the material which an exhibition has to offer. The pilot scheme is operating in three counties in western, central and northern Sweden, under local working parties, in conjunction with *A Land to Live in* (see above) and the mini-exhibition *Environment for the Million* (printed in an edition of 300).

A large proportion of the funds allocated for experiments with new forms of study have been used to equip operations and information centres, where individuals and groups can go with questions and suggestions, or requests for practical help, e.g. for photography services to help them document their own environment and conservation problems. Film shows, theatre performances, debates and lectures were also to be a feature, together with blank screens, tools and other materials to enable groups or individuals to produce their own exhibitions, posters and so on.

The State-sponsored experimental scheme for the use of radio and television in education (TRU) produced a radio and television series for adult students in 1970 entitled *We Call them Developing Countries*. To accompany it, there was an illustrated textbook and an optional exhibition produced by STE (300 copies), covering topics included in the course ('rich and poor', 'cultivation methods', 'the struggle for knowledge', 'have the developing countries a chance?' and so on), on three screens with texts, illustrations and a number of objects from the countries in question—sugar cane and a 'literacy flag' from Cuba, an earthenware vessel and printed picture of Buddha from Ceylon, a hoe from Zambia, printed cotton fabric from Tanzania. In honour of the twenty-fifth anniversary, a fourth screen was devoted to the work of the United Nations in the developing countries.

The STE experiments have already shown that the exhibition can make a major contribution to the work of schools and popular education agencies; nor would there seem to be any doubt about the valuable services which a central exhibition organization can offer the museums.

In a controversial book *Museums in the Seventies*, published in 1970, the heads of four Swedisch museums argue that the increased attendance figures are illusory, that there are not new visitors but simply more visits by the same limited selection of people that have always visited museums. This is partly attributed to the nature of the exhibitions themselves—too little staff and money being available to make them attractive enough. The authors rightly stress the need for museums to extend their influence, socially and geographically; in this regard, the exhibition is simply one instrument among many.

It is here that a central exhibition organization such as STE can provide a supplement and an alternative to the exhibitions put on by the individual museums. It is no less important that exhibitions made by museums and other bodies should reach as many people as possible, and STE has therefore devoted a great part of its resources to taking over and where necessary adapting exhibitions made by others so that they can be sent on tour round the country. A central organization also makes it easier for museums to participate in such joint productions as *A Land to Live in* (the result of an unprecedented collaboration between a museum of natural history and the Central Office of National Antiquities). STE has served as a kind of informal consultative body for museums and other exhibition makers, apart from which a certain amount of its production has taken the form of semi-manufactures for use by museums and others. Products of this kind include the 'red cabinets' (containers-cum-show-cases designed for waiting rooms and other places in need of a face-lift); information sheets on materials and methods for exhibition-making are also planned.

In co-operation with the International Council of Museums, which is sponsoring a project for training museum personal, STE is working on *A Kit on Kits*—different ways of making small exhibitions. At present the box contains samples: *How to Make a Rotten Exhibition*—(in English, since the material was first tested at the Leicester Department for Museum Studies); a 7-minute silent colour film showing small exhibitions of various kinds; a large selection of pictures and sketches; and a set of large blank cardboard screens for the students' own activities.

As an educational instrument the temporary and travelling exhibition is being employed more and more frequently all over the world. In India a mobile science museum is used to transport and exhibit exhibitions originally produced in Calcutta throughout the country. Nigeria has a mobile museum unit provided by Unesco for adult classes, dealing with modern agricultural techniques. In the United Kingdom, where travelling exhibitions were first organized by the Victoria and Albert Museum in 1855, new museum school services are rapidly expanding. In the United States, the Boston Children's Museum is working on the 'Match-Box' project (Materials and Activities for Teachers and Children).

Producing this type of exhibition, designed for use in teaching over relatively long periods, demands staff, money and time. Exchanges of experience and information are particularly valuable; opportunities are provided by the ICOM conferences and publications (including the new *ICOM Annual*, which deals specifically with museum education). Apart from its publication of *Museum* and the *Unesco Courier*, Unesco could perhaps help by sponsoring international exchanges of small exhibitions, slides, films and other pictorial material and by arranging contacts through such interesting projects as the Associated Schools Project in Education—an excellent forum for exhibition-makers the world over.

Reaching a distant public

8

The Moscow Polytechnic Museum celebrates its centenary in December 1972. It was founded by leading Russian scholars of the Amateur Natural Sciences, Anthropology and Ethnography Society, which was responsible for the All-Russian Polytechnic Exhibition in 1872 from which the museum grew. This was the first museum for the people, and it was open to everyone.

Its very large collections cover the key sectors of industry: mining, metallurgy, engineering, cars, chemistry, physics, energetics, radio-electronics, automation, computer technology and astronautics. Actual machinery or models and apparatus, equipment, instruments, raw materials and finished products explain the principles underlying the major technological processes.

The eighty rooms contain over 25,000 exhibits. Some are unique, for example the first electric motors invented by B. S. Yakobi and M. O. Dolivo-Dobrovolsky, the electric plug invented by P. N. Yablochkov, S. S. Popov's radio receiver and the telegraphic apparatus invented by P. L. Shilling.

Since 1947, the museum has been the headquarters of the All-Union Society for the Dissemination of Scientific and Technical Information ('Znanie').

Every visitor to the museum will find much that is new, useful and interesting. But what about those who live far from Moscow?

K. Vilenskaya is Deputy Director of the Moscow Polytechnic Museum, and B. Agafoshina is Head of the Methods Department.

For them, the museum organizes travelling exhibitions which considerably extend its scope, enabling it to reach the remotest corners of the land. At present, it operates twenty; five or six new exhibitions being introduced annually to replace ones that are going out of date. Each visits from four to six towns of varying size annually, remaining one or two months in each.

The exhibitions are organized in co-operation with the appropriate ministries, institutes, firms and societies. Exhibitions are of various kinds:

Popular science exhibitions: new trends in science and technology; for visitors of all categories, e.g. *The Role of Chemistry in the National Economy, Semi-conductors and their Application, Radio-electronics in the Service of Man.*

Specialized exhibitions, for specific categories of experts, e.g. *Polymers in Building, Semi-conductor Converters, Curved Sections—A New Progress in Metal-rolling.*

Popular science exhibitions on technical developments, e.g. *The Development of Astronautics in the U.S.S.R.*

Exhibitions of items belonging to the museum.

An annotated list of travelling exhibitions is circulated to all interested organizations. Exhibitions are then sent on request to technical or cultural clubs, firms, institutes, museums, social centres and parks.

Exhibitions dealing with modern science and technology are most in demand. Consequently, each section of the museum prepares

Atoms for Peace exhibition, Bratislava, 1966.

Travelling exhibition: *Astronautics in the U.S.S.R.,* Dresden, March 1970.

Travelling exhibition: *Radio-electronics in the Service of Man,* displayed in towns throughout the Soviet Union, 1966.

Travelling exhibition: *Synthetic Glues and Methods of Adhesion,* displayed in towns across the Soviet Union, 1969. ▶

Lenin Centenary Travelling Exhibition: Lenin's ideas for the electrification of the land of the Soviets; Prague, April 1970.

a travelling exhibition on developments in its particular branch, in liaison with the industrial and research institutes that can provide information, instruments, samples, or finished products for exhibition purposes. The information is processed and sent in the form of an 'exhibition subject plan', together with diagrammatic and illustrative material, to the design studios for final production. Meanwhile, a brochure is compiled and published. A member of the section concerned travels with the exhibition to supervise its mounting and give any advice needed.

Travelling exhibitions need an area of from 50 to 200 square metres. With rare exceptions, only two men are needed for the loading, unloading and assembly, so that exhibitions can visit places which have no special handling equipment. For certain large-scale exhibitions (e.g. *Atoms for Peace* needing 400–500 square metres), special transport and equipment were needed. A full-time expert from the museum was assigned to this exhibition, and remained with it all the time it was on show.

Organized tours are arranged for schoolchildren, students, teachers and other groups. Advisory services are provided for specialists. Meetings on various subjects, to which experts and teachers from outlying areas are invited, are usually held in connexion with the exhibition which, as a result of publicity in the local press, radio and television, is visited by people from all walks of life.

In 1951, eight travelling exhibitions were on display in and around Moscow; in 1969, twenty-two were operating in forty-eight towns in the Soviet Union.

Chemistry has had a large place in the exhibitions because of the rapid development of the synthetic polymer industry and the importance of chemistry in all sectors of the national economy.

The introduction of new chemical substances into various branches of industry and agriculture largely depended on the speed with which information about them reached remote parts of the country. There was a good deal of prejudice against synthetic materials, and the exhibitions helped to dispel it. One on *Polymers in the National Economy*, consisting of posters, diagrams, graphs, photographs and a large collection of samples, explained to visitors the main physical and chemical properties of the new synthetic materials and articles manufactured from them, their multiple uses, their economic advantages and future production prospects. Lectures by a specialist from the museum and films on polymers from the local film library enhanced the effect—together with the possibility of handling the actual exhibits.

This exhibition was on show for two years in the Far East, Central Asia, and in many towns in northern and European Russia. Among those who specially benefited from it were chemistry teachers living in remote areas.

Two years after this exhibition for the general public, the following more specialized exhibitions on polymers were organized by the chemistry section: *Synthetic Glues and Methods of Adhesion*; *Polymer Materials in Building*; *The Use of Fluoroplastics (Teflon) in Technology*. The layout was similar to that used in the popular exhibition, but the theoretical side and manufacture and processing technology were dealt with more fully; a list of factories making polymers was also provided.

Exhibitions of this kind in technical clubs and in the design rooms in factories always attract a lot of entries—opinions and suggestions—in the visitors' book.

The most popular of the history of technology exhibitions was *The History of Astronautics* which traced the developments underlying space flights from the work of the pioneer of Soviet astronautics, K. E. Tsiolkovsky, to man's walk in space.

An interesting variation is offered during the summer by travelling exhibitions on river boats. One on radio-electronics in 1964 was on display for a month, travelling on the Volga and Oka rivers, and stopping at almost all populated places.

During the past decade, the museum has taken an active part in international programmes. Under scientific and cultural cooperation agreements, it exchanges exhibitions with museums in the socialist countries, a valuable way of pooling experience which also affords opportunities for studying methods used in similar establishments abroad.

The first exhibition abroad was *Hydroelectric Construction*, shown at the Prague National Technical Museum, in 1958. In 1963, the *Atoms for Peace* exhibition was on show, subsequently visiting almost all the larger cities of the U.S.S.R. In 1966, *What is Automation?* was displayed at the Warsaw Museum of Science and Technology. In its turn, Prague sent to Moscow *From the Rushlight to the Contemporary Fluorescent Lamp*, and Warsaw sent *From Copernicus to the Space Flights*, which was later shown with great success in many Soviet cities.

In view of the interest of such exchanges for the museums themselves and for the public, the directors of four technical museums in Prague, Dresden, Warsaw, Moscow, decided in 1960 to organize a joint exhibition: *Technical Museums and their Contribution to the Polytechnic Education of Youth*. This opened in Warsaw in 1967. Warsaw covered man's efforts to master various forms of energy; Prague, man's use of stone, and the development of sound recording from Edison's phonograph to the stereophonic tape recorder; Dresden dealt with the history of photography; and Moscow, museum work with schools, including programmed instruction. Shown in turn, over a four-year period, in Warsaw, Prague, Dresden and Moscow, it reached the Moscow Polytechnic Museum in 1970, where it aroused great interest among scientists and teachers alike.

Symposia held in each of the cities were attended by representatives from the ministries of education, museums and the teaching profession who discussed ways and means of further enhancing the contribution of technical museums and travelling exhibitions to polytechnic education in the socialist countries. Together with the omnipresent cinema, radio and television, they will remain a potent means of education that can be made still more effective by exchanges of experience and joint exhibitions.

Mahmoud Mesallam Hassan

The exhibitions a developing country needs

9

Children can go to schools and universities to prepare themselves for a future and better life, but many of the grown-ups have missed that opportunity. They are either completely illiterate or have very little education. As they are important parts of a living system working for economic development, educational services should be devoted to them. If villagers are to be healthy and strong, they need to know about diseases and carriers of diseases —which of course affect production. Farmers need new ideas about farming, irrigation, drainage, pest control, cattle-raising, fertilizers. Fishermen need to know more about the sea, the weather, the behaviour and habits of fish, new methods and techniques. Workers need to know more about machines—how to use them and protect themselves against their dangers.

Developing countries have had their own civilizations. They have contributed much to man's knowledge. The young should know this bright history and accept the challenge to emulate it.

Nothing can help more than museums, which now are living institutions that can offer invaluable educational services to the new public. But museums need special buildings, a special design and much space. They cost a lot and need much effort and experience. If a developing country can afford to establish a museum it will usually be in the capital and thus confined to a limited public.

Mahmoud Mesallam Hassan is Director, Museum of Science and Technology, Cairo.

The importance of travelling and temporary exhibitions becomes evident.

As people differ in their cultural levels and needs, travelling exhibitions can be either specific or general.

Specific exhibitions can be designed for schoolchildren, villagers, workers and fishermen.

Exhibitions for schoolchildren should help them in mastering the curriculum. This does not mean that exhibits should stick exactly to what is written in their books, but should rather help them to extend the horizon of their knowledge.

In science exhibitions, exhibits are preferably of a kind that arouse the interest of the child and set him thinking. He pushes a button and something interesting happens. This awakens his curiosity. He tries to find the explanation. If he fails, a demonstrator appears and gives the hint that allows him another chance to think. He may pass through a hall, and find his hair standing on end, or come near a mirror which whistles. He can make different musical tones by moving his fingers near the mirror ... children learn much through playing.

The exhibits should be so arranged as to tell a complete story. To counteract space problems some may be designed to demonstrate more than one scientific principle, e.g. the behaviour of light rays (reflection and refraction), and the spectrum, can be demonstrated by one simple exhibit such as a rotating disc in a dark case on which different lenses, prisms and mirrors are mounted.

Mahmoud Mesallam Hassan

Visitors to an exhibition.

A village exhibition on fighting disease.

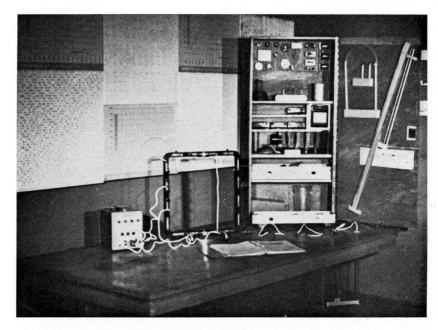

An educational exhibition, simply designed and
very easy to mount.

Chemistry kit on loan to junior schools.

The space available in a school or elsewhere in a village or small town seldom exceeds 200 square metres. As the exhibits should tell a complete story, the exhibition should concentrate on one subject only. The question then is whether it will be possible to have more than one exhibition in a particular area in a year so as to cover more than one subject. But whatever the number, it will be almost impossible to cover the subject fully in this way.

To overcome this difficulty in Egypt, science centres have been set up in the principal cities. These are like small science museums and send out travelling exhibitions, each covering a specific subject, to the surrounding towns and villages. These exhibitions can be easily exchanged, as the exhibits are simply designed and can be mounted within a few hours.

School exhibitions are accompanied by film shows, coloured slides, and film-strips. Lectures with demonstrations are given daily during the exhibition. Popular books are available. Children are encouraged to consult them and write reports and short essays on subjects that interest them Prizes are awarded for the best reports and essays.

The science centres have science kits with which the teacher can demonstrate over eighty experiments in physics and mechanics, and the chemistry experiments needed in junior schools; kits dealing with local minerals and rocks; kits for collectors of minerals, rocks, crystals and fossils; boxes for insects (explaining their life cycle); boxes for local reptiles, birds and some mammals, and so on. Schools are allowed these kits and boxes on loan for two weeks each.

To carry out this scheme, teachers are selected for training at summer courses, and specialists are assigned to the work annually by the government.

The exhibits for villagers must be largely self-explanatory, use very few words, be closely related to their needs and help them to increase production.

The following flow of exhibits for fighting diseases is suggested:

Dangers to life that diseases represent. These should be underlined to create a strong impression and a determination to keep away from them.

How people become infected. The life cycles of parasites must be explained.

How to protect against infection.

What governments are doing to help them in fighting diseases; research in laboratories and in the field, new drugs being manufactured at home and abroad.

Egypt has had many exhibitions of this kind and many others are in preparation.

In bilharzia exhibitions, for example, the first exhibit explains the dangers by means of post-mortem specimens of enlarged liver, enlarged spleen, cancer-infected bladder and lungs, and so on, and lighted transparencies showing how sick people look when infected.

The second exhibit explains how infection occurs. Good dioramas showing a canal, in which children are swimming, passing through a village; women are washing clothes and vegetables; farmers are getting water by different means to irrigate their farms with their bare feet in the canal. The different stages of the life cycle are shown in magnified wax or plastic models, together with a collection of molluscs, slides on which worms are mounted, and a microscope.

The third exhibit explains the methods of protection: dioramas show chemicals used for getting rid of molluscs, killing the plants on which molluscs stick, different kinds of sprayers, drugs and injections used for treatment.

National history has its part. Drawings and writings from ancient Egyptian tombs show that no one could go to Paradise in the hereafter if he once polluted water. All Egyptians when about to die had to swear before the priest that they had never killed, never stolen and never polluted water. Again a prescription for the treatment of bilharzia written over 4,000 years ago is shown, together with a modern prescription to show the near resemblance. The tomb in which bilharzia was first discovered, and the work of Ibn Sina, the Arab scientist who was the first to discover bilharzia and to write about it, also form part of the exhibit.

This exhibition makes a very strong impression on people. A symposium on bilharzia is held each year in a village. The Science Museum takes part, as each symposium is accompanied by an exhibition dealing mainly with bilharzia. A committee of the youth of the village selected is set up to discuss the problems of bilharzia and other diseases, under the guidance of specialists. Every week the members see films about diseases and how they are spread. The films are very simple, in colour, and rely on cartoons and comedy. The members of this committee become the demonstrators at the exhibition. They speak to the people in language they can understand.

Plays, songs and dances prepared by specialists and artists are performed by the villagers themselves and well-known artists. This has proved very successful and has helped research, since people had confidence and felt friendly towards those who had come to them to help and advise.

Something not less important; teachers were asked to concentrate on bilharzia in their drawing, composition, arithmetic and science lessons. Children wrote on the plays, the films they had seen and the exhibition they had visited. The result of this experiment was the complete disappearance of bilharzia from the village.

Exhibitions are arranged for farmers to help to increase the productivity of the land and the farmer's income. The exhibitions are based on the following subjects:

New methods of irrigation and their advantages over the old—they can cover vast areas with water in a short time and help to protect against certain parasitic worms.

The exact amount of water needed in a specific area for a specific crop. This helps to save much water.

The importance of drainage for desalting the land, and the advantages of covered drainage, which increases the area available for cultivation and diminishes the risks of infection.

The importance of dams for storing water.

The importance of fertilizers—kinds, samples, where and when they are used.

Best methods of storing cereals.

Collections of insects which attack plants and damage crops. Samples of chemicals used in insect control.

Collections of local birds which feed on destructive insects and can be friends to farmers.

Other collections of birds which cause damage. How to protect crops from them.

Samples of seeds varieties, their yields, and ability to resist fungi.

Cross-breeding to produce new and better varieties.

Varieties of poultry and cattle, and the advantages of each.

Diseases that may attack farm animals. Methods of protection.

Healthy accommodation for poultry and cattle raising.

Bees as honey producers and carriers of pollen (so increasing plant productivity).

Uses of plant and animal waste.

As for general exhibitions, these are usually intended for the general public, and cover (a) big national projects and their importance in helping to increase the national income; or (b) social or technological advances, national and international. The following are some examples which were very successful in Egypt.

Energy: (a) nuclear (what are atoms, unstable atoms and radioactivity, samples of radioactive minerals, detection of nuclear radiations, fusion and fission, nuclear reactors, accelerators); (b) solar (how solar energy is produced, uses of solar energy [cooking, baking, drying fruit and vegetables, water heating, generation of electricity, melting metals, producing fresh water from salt water]); (c) electrical (production of electricity, power stations [hydraulic, thermal,

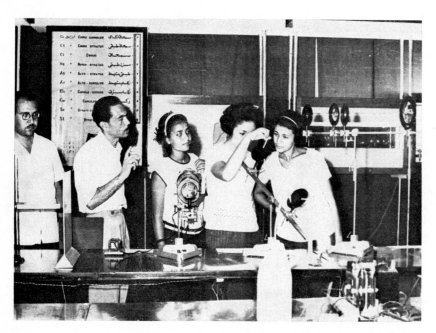

Physics and mechanics loan kit for junior schools.

Travelling exhibition of chemicals used for insect control.

Nuclear-energy exhibition: fusion and fission,
nuclear reactors.

Exhibition on the practical use of solar energy
for heating water.

Exhibition on production of electric energy.

Mechanical energy—windmill for raising underground water and for the production of electricity.

nuclear], transfer of electricity, transformers and uses in melting and welding, kinds of electric current), effects of electric current and uses (electromagnets, electroplating, heaters); (d) thermal (fuels—heat produced from each in calories per gramme, combustion engines); (e) mechanical (energy from wind, lifting underground water, production of electricity, driving boats, driving clouds from over the oceans and seas to land).

Natural resources: (a) mineral (samples of minerals, localities where found); (b) plant (textile, medical, food-producing, oil-producing, wood-producing); (c) animal (industries depending on various animal resources, projects for new industries, models of factories).

Electronics in our life: what is an electron?, valves, electromagnetic waves, transistors, radio and television, radar, computers.

Exhibits are made to entertain and educate, and should be continually reviewed by educators who study their influence, notice which exhibits attract and which fail, and listen to the comments of people to find out why.

From my own experience I think most people are interested in working models, and most of our exhibits were changed accordingly. If photos are necessary, colour transparencies should be used, with changing or moving lights. Statistics should not be in lines or curves but in shapes and volumes. Long, written explanations are worse than useless—the exhibit should be so designed that a few simple words suffice to explain its purpose.

Children can easily be influenced and like to do things by themselves. To give them opportunities, the science centres mentioned above also serve as clubs in which they can practise hobbies.

Many important occasions and events, national and international, are worthy of celebration: the anniversary of the foundation of an old city; the anniversary of a liberator, scientist, socialist, writer or artist;

the completion of a major national project; brilliant achievements in science and technology; and so on. Temporary exhibitions are usually arranged to mark such occasions.

In an exhibition celebrating the anniversary of the foundation of a city, each period should have its own period decorations, so that the visitor feels he is physically witnessing its contemporary life. Exhibits should show the social life during the successive periods, medical, scientific and artistic achievements, relations with surrounding countries, wars, the leaders who won victory, forts built for defence, weapons used, how wars bring destruction and stop development and progress while co-operation means living in peace and higher standards of living.

A temporary exhibition for a famous man is usually held in the place where he was born. The exhibits should tell all about his life, his paintings or writings, tools or apparatus, the places where he lived and worked, what he contributed to mankind.

Most museums have special halls for temporary exhibitions. People like to know what other peoples do or have done. Temporary exhibitions thus travel from one country to another. The exhibition on Tutankhamen, the ancient Egyptian king, with his gold tomb and other treasures, which was seen in various cities in the United States and in France during the last few years, is a good example of an excellent form of cultural co-operation between the nations.

Temporary exhibitions to mark the completion of a big national project or a brilliant scientific and technical achievement make a deep impression on the public. Tax-payers should know everything about such projects or achievements; the facts are the fuel that stimulates enthusiasm and paves the way for the success of other such projects in future.

Most of the museum personnel in developing countries lack the kind of experience necessary in preparing travelling exhibitions. Trainees sent abroad can visit museums, but these museums seldom have practical training courses. Frankly, trainees do not benefit very much, and those coming back home have not enough experience to carry out the big job properly.

Unesco should encourage the advanced countries to hold symposia and conferences periodically in the developing countries, at which designs for exhibits prepared by international experts could be discussed, together with such questions as translating ideas into exhibits, how to display exhibits, and how to preserve them. The developing countries need these exchanges of experience, and a periodical injection of new ideas.

W. Stephen Thomas

How do museums use the mass media?

10

A report from the United States

The museum, once aloof and remote, is radically changing, developing a social conscience; seeking to be of value and use to everyone. Museums are attracting more and more visitors—more, sometimes, in the United States, than they can conveniently handle. Some thirty years ago, 50 million visits were paid annually to 2,000 museums. In 1969, the figure had grown to over 300 million visits, and new museums are increasing at the rate of six every seven days. Nevertheless, many segments of both urban and rural communities are not yet reached.

In attempting to reach them, museums can use radio, television, the press and films in addition to such other means as tapes, slides, prints, reproductions, publications, reports and catalogues.

This article derives from a working paper 'The Museum as a Communicator' submitted to an ICOM symposium in Paris in November 1964 and published as an appendix to *Museums and the Education of Adults*.[1]

To bring the material up to date, questionnaires (69 questions) on the use of radio, television, press and films were sent in June 1970 to 200 museums in 35 States of the United States. Replies were received from 133 (66.4 per cent).

RADIO

In the United States in 1968 there were 216 million radio sets in 59.8 million homes (over three times the number of black-and-white and ten times the number of colour television receivers), as well as 74 million radios in automobiles. Radio has the advantage over television in that people can listen to radio while doing other things. Factory and other workers, housewives and drivers listen for hours every day.

A survey of 2,538 United States museums made by the Office of Education in 1966 showed that 4.5 per cent produced their own regular radio programmes. The author's recent study showed that 12 per cent of the 133 museums which replied had regular radio programmes but 75 per cent used radio only for spot announcements.[2] Radio stations welcome news and information from museums and have it read by announcers in varying amounts but at frequent intervals on commercial or educational channels. Museums large enough to have public-relations specialists

W. Stephen Thomas is Director, Development and Public Affairs, Rochester Museum and Science Center, United States.

1. Hans Zetterberg (ed.), *Museums and the Education of Adults*, London, Evelyn & Adams, 1968.
2. Lola Eriksen Rogers, *Museums and Related Institutions: A Basic Program Survey*, Washington, D.C., United States Department of Health, Education and Welfare, 1969.

on their staffs, especially if located in the larger cities, had their news items used daily, or at least five days each week. In cities with four or more stations, museum information was broadcast by radio many times daily. As for features other than news, the interview with a staff member was used in 56 per cent of the cases reported, lecture-type programmes in only 12 per cent.

Of museums employing radio for both information and educational purposes, 70 per cent broadcast through local commercial and 31 per cent through local educational channels; 11.2 per cent had the advantage of regional or national networks. Estimated audiences ranged from 3,000–5,000 to 30,000–50,000 in larger cities; six museums reported 50,000 or more, and museums in San Diego and Cincinnati reported 1 million and 1.5 million respectively.

A children's museum in New England commented:

Radio is the most rapid and effective method of getting out a change of plans and programmes which are suddenly to be given on holidays or when bad weather comes. On the coverage of events of scientific interest such as the finding of dinosaur tracks or special news events such as appearances of copper-head snakes, etc., television is excellent but not so accessible.

The Baltimore Museum of Art said:

We can observe a clear relationship between coverage of museum events and activities [by radio] and an increased attendance and participation in museum programmes.

One museum in the south-west broadcasts interviews and lectures by staff members and gets a better response through them to announcements of new exhibits, shows, and so on, than through the press.

A small but effective children's museum writes:

For spot announcements the radio stations seek us out for information and edit material from announcements in our bulletins which we send them, leaving us with little or no work, but getting the same results as if we had prepared the releases and announcements.

The Dallas Health and Science Museum reports that the local radio stations give considerable free coverage daily to their exhibits, planetarium shows and educational courses.

Among the many interesting examples of museum-radio relations were the National Gallery of Art in Washington *Picture of the Week* broadcasts (until 1967) during the intervals in its public concerts. An expert usually discussed a great painting. To assist listeners in following the discussion, the gallery offered reproductions of each painting, on paper suitable for framing. Talks and interviews are now broadcast from the gallery on a variety of subjects. The conductor of the National Gallery Orchestra usually gives a three-minute talk about the current concert. This is followed by a ten-minute programme on such subjects as 'Twentieth Century British Graphic Art', 'Art in the Service of the Court', 'Some Equestrian Statues in Washington', 'What is a Minor Master?', 'Religious Art'.[1]

It is estimated that in 62 per cent of museums the staff plan and write the scripts; only 28 per cent use professional radio personnel and, even then, sometimes use them only in collaboration.

It can thus be seen that, despite the more spectacular qualities of television, radio has specific advantages for museums as an educational and information medium. Radio programmes are cheaper to produce, need less staff and do not as a rule involve the handling of valuable museum objects; if they have news value they may be more easily used and hence, more freely accepted. And programme time is contributed free by most local stations.

1. 'Museums Seek Audiences Through Radio Concerts', *Arts Management* No. 31, October 1964; and a letter from Jane J. Wallace, Public Information Office, National Gallery of Art, 13 October 1970, Washington, D.C.

TELEVISION

In the last twenty years, museums have increasingly sought more effective means of making their riches known to huge audiences. For this, in the United States, television has proved best, although its use for this purpose is still relatively limited. Of 133 museums suveyed, 82 per cent use television in some form, 60 per cent regularly using spot announcements, 12 per cent having their own regular programmes, lasting from 15 to 30 minutes.

As early as 1946, staff of a museum appeared as guests on television. In the next year, this museum pioneered several experimental programmes. In 1948 the Milwaukee Museum had a travel and history programme for young people. In 1950, the University Museum in Philadelphia started a highly influential weekly feature, *What in the World?* A panel of experts were shown ancient or primitive artefacts or other puzzling objects and asked to guess their identity, use and approximate date. As viewers were told in advance what the object was and the specialists were remarkably bright, the programme was both instructive and amusing. It proved so successful that it was put on a national network and survived for eight years. The British Broadcasting Corporation followed suit with *Animal, Vegetable or Mineral?*, with Sir Mortimer Wheeler, Director of the British Academy, as Master of Ceremonies.

Successful network programmes broadcast by several of the larger museums in the 1950s included the award-winning *Adventure* (American Museum of Natural History in New York City). Continuing from 1951 to 1954, it took viewers on explorations

... into wild and little-known parts of the world, re-enacted the birth of the earth and showed the development of life on it, subjects as high and wide as the solar system, the complex composition of a hen's egg, what animals can see, the cultural crisis of the Navajo Indian, and the cause of thunderstorms.[1]

In its first year, thirty-five scientists from the museum's own staff appeared on the programme as well as many other specialists. At the height of its popularity the series was viewed regularly by 3 million people. The Milwaukee Museum engaged a television co-ordinator in 1952. After a series of experiments, the four types of programmes decided upon proved popular and successful.

The *Explorers' Club* for children worked in conjunction with a children's programme at the museum, and the *Explorers' Log* was circulated to thousands during the year. *Let's Experiment* centred on a friendly scientist working in a museum laboratory, demonstrating basic principles in physics and chemistry with everything from bicycles and ice-cream to jet planes. These demonstrations supplemented the natural history adventures of the *Explorers' Club*. At first the physics broadcasts were less popular, but when 'more fun and excitement, simple experiments to do at home and a small boy to help the scientist were added, to spark its appeal', the programme became highly successful.

A large family audience was found for *Diorama* (originally called *Hobby Hall*). This programme at first featured amateurs and their science, history, handicrafts and other occupations. The change of title came when it ceased to confine itself to hobbies and began to cover wider cultural and public issues.

The World to You dealt with the local implications of scientific or historical topics.

No Doubt About It was a quiz programme on 'mystery objects' selected from the museum's collections.[2]

Commenting upon the experiment, Robert E. Dierbeck, wrote:

1. Edward Wyer, *Natural History,* June 1954.
2. Leon W. Weissgerber, 'All About "No Doubt About It", Panel Quiz Program of Milwaukee Public Museum', *Curator,* Vol. IV, No. 41961.

The natural differences in the methods of television, with its tendency toward the 'bold', broad strokes of Madison Avenue, and the museum with its preference for quiet restraint and thoughtful precision, presented understandable difficulties. But, as the professional scientist learned the values of showmanship, the professional broadcaster gained an increasing respect for scholarship. Methods were developed to set the dramatic highlight against the background of solid information, to check extreme erudition with popular appeal, and to maintain accuracy in spite of simplification and focus. The result was highly effective museum television.[1]

By 1956, eighty-two of the larger museums had a television activity of some sort; fifty had actually produced programmes but only ten had a full season (thirty-nine weekly programmes).[2] In 1964 a survey by the American Association of Museums showed that some thirty-five museums were using television fairly intensively, but usually only through spots on commercial and educational channels.[3]

Our most recent survey (see above) shows that the number of museums producing their own programmes has shrunk to only 17 of the 133 questioned. Former producers which have dropped out during the last two or three years include the California Academy of Sciences, Buffalo Museum and Erie County Historical Society, the Denver Art Museum and the American Museum of Natural History. Although the programmes were successful, most museums found that it cost too much to engage professionals; or that it took too much of staff time to plan programmes, select the material, and write the scripts; or that they had no witty expert available with the special personality needed in the master of ceremonies who puts its programme across.

Of the remainder, one of the most successful is the Boston Museum of Fine Arts, which has four full-time television staff. They broadcast two weekly half-hour programmes, *Images* and *Museum Open House*, with a total of sixty-eight programmes a season (including some repeats). After paying $100,000 to wire the galleries, the annual budget is about $35,000.

Once a theme was decided upon (e.g. the contrast between ancient Greek and present-day concepts in art), the rather complicated but worth-while production procedure was as follows. The various museum departments were consulted; lighting and security arrangements were made; and information was compiled on the particular works of art to be used, together with the literary and historical references. As the speaker wrote his own script, there were frequent conferences with the producer to ensure that the final draft made good television. A television bus with mobile control-room and video-taping unit came to the museum, taking at least half a day for rehearsal and sometimes twelve hours for the actual production. The programme was pre-recorded on video tape not only to prevent last-minute blunders but because it allows immediate play-back and preparation in segments.[4]

The estimated 45,000 local viewers of *Museum Open House* each Monday night was only a fraction of the total audience. The show was seen simultaneously on the Eastern Educational Network from coast to coast, i.e. a weekly audience of hundreds of thousands. Patricia Bernard writes:

In Boston, the programmes are aired in prime evening time. We are addressing the adult viewer whose interests prompt him to tune in an educational station, at least occasionally, but he doesn't necessarily have any knowledge of art history. At the first hint of boredom he will shift

1. Robert E. Dierbeck, 'Television and the Museum', *Curator*, No. 2, 1958, p. 38.
2. Sherman P. Lawton, *Museum Television Survey Report*, Norman, Okla., University of Oklahoma, 1958.
3. W. Stephen Thomas, 'The Museum as Communicator', *The Museologist*, Rochester, N.Y., March 1965.
4. Patricia Bernard, 'Problems and Techniques on Producing Museum Programmes', *Museum News*, Vol. 45, No. 7, March 1967, p. 35 to 39.

channels or pick up a good book. Holding him is a challenge. We feel that the visual experience is primary—interesting camera work on the works of art, but beyond that we feel that the speaker must be a performer, must have personal magnetism. . . .[1]

The present author's analysis showed that 72 per cent of museums used the interview type of programme in preference to panel discussions and lectures; 60 per cent used museum objects, usually insisting that they be handled only by museum personnel, and avoiding fragile material as much as possible. As in radio, the frequency of programmes varied from spot announcements several days a week to as low as a few times a year.

Few museums replied to the question regarding the audience sought, but a majority aimed at both adults and children.

Local commercial stations were used by 70 per cent; 47 per cent used educational channels; a few used both. There is an increasing preference for educational channels, however. These stations are interested in local cultural institutions as sources, and have more time available on the air; moreover, foundations and state governments (especially New York) are subsidizing educational television by museums.

The following are some of the views expressed by representative museums throughout the country.

The California Academy of Sciences:

The six local stations give us very generous public service time—both with 35 mm colour slides (with voice over) as well as 10-second motion picture spots. . . . Our *Science in Action* television show was on television for 15 years. We cannot any longer afford to present it—though it was singularly successful.

Starting with closed-circuit television for schools, sponsored by the Travelers Insurance Co., the Hartford Children's Museum in Connecticut began a new and imaginative television series in 1957, using its own collections and staff. It developed into a twenty-minute series called *Alive and About*, broadcast for twenty-six weeks, first in 1963/64, and eventually broadcast by twenty-two stations in 1968/69 from Maine to Virginia and west to Chicago.[2]

The Columbus Museum of Arts and Crafts in Georgia:

Materials from interesting exhibits are shown on television as such exhibits are booked; also, some art exhibits are discussed and paintings shown. Occasional film strips on these are made by the television station, as well as on new permanent exhibits.

At the Albright-Knox Art Gallery in Buffalo, the Curator of Education took part in a programme for children called *Let's Go to the Art Gallery* from June to October 1967. Paintings and sculpture in the gallery's collection were discussed with the children.

The Charlotte Nature Museum in North Carolina:

We have weekly appearances with artefacts or live animals on two commercial television stations, plus irregular half-hour shows on our local educational television channel.

The Cincinnati Art Museum:

Our television coverage by spot announcements, news broadcasts and general programmes usually is most concentrated at times of exhibition openings when there may be four stations using materials at the same time.

The Granbrook Institute of Science in Michigan co-operated in a ten-week series. Five of the staff were each responsible for two 30-minute programmes. They were interviewed by professional television personnel.

It may be well in conclusion to mention a few pointers on museum television planning by a director of university radio and television, T. Ellsworth Stepp of the University of Colorado:

1. ibid., p. 37.
2. Mrs Jane M. B. Cheney, 'A Museum's Experience in Television Production', *The Museologist*, September 1970, p. 24.

You will soon discover that one of the largest problems in a television programme is the person or persons you will use. . . . It doesn't make any difference how good your material is, if the personality does not come across, you'll end up with what the people in the industry call a 'dog' of a programme. . . . Depending of course, on the type of programme, I have found it is usually better not to work from a complete script. This is because you will probably be working with people who are not professionals and as a result they will sound as if they were reading. . . . Another important consideration in planning a programme is that of content. . . . Almost without exception there are too many subjects to be presented. More material can be presented on television than radio because you have the added advantage of the visual factor. However, it is still true that usually the simpler the show is, the better it is. . . .[1]

THE PRESS

Despite all, the daily newspaper remains perhaps the museum's most reliable outlet for information and popular education. There were 1,752 daily newspapers in the English language in the United States in 1969, with a combined circulation of 62,535,394; and all museums, no matter how small, have news which can be used in the local press.

Radio and television may reach more people, but the local newspaper is a steady and reliable user of a wide range of local news, and even if only one person in each family reads the papers, information spreads rapidly by word of mouth.

Most newspapers are willing to use museum material, but only in rare cases do reporters and columnists have the time to dig out their own stories. Hence the museum must itself be alert, not simply waiting for news to happen but in many cases anticipating what may happen and be newsworthy. Using the telephone is perfectly legitimate, but daily and weekly newspapers and house and monthly magazines can be reached more efficiently by press releases. These should be as simple as possible, resume the relevant facts, use proper names where significant, and always remember the potentiel user's tastes and interests.

The opening of a new exhibition nearly always provides a good story (referred to by 95 per cent of museums in the survey). Next in popularity is the interview (81 per cent) with a foreign or out-of-town dignitary, expert, speaker or lecturer. The press is nearly always glad to interview the archaeologist when he returns from his dig, the biologist back from his expedition or the museum trustee with something interesting to say about museum laboratory projects or new exhibits.

Almost equally popular is the news or a new gift or purchase, or programmes and events in which the public can participate.

. . . Evaluate your event with the eye of a reporter. Scholarly facts and details should be included, yes! But they should not be the things the editor is expected to hang his headlines to. Look for interest, look for the unusual. . . .[2]

Obviously, the straight news story is the one easiest to place and the one most welcomed by editors (81 per cent of the museum favoured this type). But a variety of items other than those mentioned above can produce news of sufficient value to be printed: new buildings, plans for additions, new policy, new public services, staff changes (of local interest in smaller towns).

Again, there are the writers of columns and special sections. Society editors, especially in women's and family papers, know the value

---

1. T. Ellsworth Stepp, 'Planning Museum Television Programmes', *Clearing House for Western Museums*, p. 726, Denver, Colo., September 1954 (Newsletter 175).
2. William Morrison, 'Your Public Relations Cards', *Museum News*, January 1963, p. 11.

of names. Newspapers in larger cities usually carry weekly articles on art criticism and often depend on museums for material; writers on bird-lore, animals and plant-life use information which natural-history and science museums can easily supply. With the new interest in ecology and the environment, newspapers rely more and more on museum scientists and educators. Community programmes in conservation education, now becoming popular, are often helped, or even started, by museum staff.

Sympathetic editors can occasionally be supplied with facts which they will incorporate in editorials. Letters to the papers can be used to publicize issues or subjects, or to rebut unfair, misleading or misinformed criticism (editors will sometimes spontaneously invite museum officials to reply).

The following are some recent comments on museum-press relations. A children's museum in New England:

We have always had remarkably good press relations. We are used as the first port of call for information on all local phenomena . . .

The Henry Francis DuPont Museum in Winterthur, Delaware:

We use the national daily press in the promotion of 'Winterthur in the Spring' and 'Winterthur in the Autumn'. Numbers of persons reached is in the millions.

The Kansas State Historical Society in Topeka:

We cultivate a working relationship with an individual reporter and suggest story ideas to him. We also help him research items that will not feature the museum. Thus, they want to keep our good-will.

The Baltimore Museum of Art:

Press coverage seems to reach a consistently larger audience with resultant increase in museum attendance.

The Museum of Fine Arts in Boston:

The estimated number of persons reached by press media is three million regularly.

The Buffalo and Erie County Historical Society:

A thorough system of press releases, telephone follow-up and personal contact has produced excellent coverage of the Society's programme.

To balance these highly favourable comments, some scepticism is expressed. A west coast science museum:

The press is an uncertain medium as to what they pick up and how they use it.

A large State Museum:

Newspaper coverage is unpredictable, depending upon the volume of competition for space by other news and advertising.

However, this is offset by the National Gallery of Art in Washington:

Our major emphasis in public relations is on the press—magazines and newspapers.

To summarize: (a) museums can be news which, in turn, makes people aware of their purpose and activities; (b) as cultural community centres, museums have an interest which is recognized by the press; (c) newspapers provide community bulletin boards, alerting people about exhibits, lectures, films, classes, concerts and other activities.

FILMS

Films have long been used by museums to supplement labels, gallery talks and other devices. It has been pointed out that film

which can truly be termed an exhibition in motion, is admirably fitted to appeal to present-day visitors, especially to young people.[1]

Unfortunately, despite the demand, such films can seldom be seen in the commercial cinema, and museums do not use them enough either.

According to a survey made by the American Association of Museums in 1963, 700 museums were using films regularly in their educational programmes, but mostly to provide a general background only rather than to illustrate specific subjects. Some museums use educational films to attract the public.

The exhibitions attract people who already know the museum and have some knowledge of art. But there are still larger numbers who must be taught where the museum is, brought past the doors and reassured in their diffidence and timidity. The best device we have discovered is the familiar motion picture, programmes of documentaries on art whenever possible, but others, too. Once inside, many people are attracted to the other resources of the museum and eventually acquire the habit of museum going.[2]

An exactly opposite point of view has also been expressed:

Films should be used only to supplement the significant object story. Museums should utilize films as an integral part of their interpretive story, rather than develop what is sometimes called strong attraction motion picture programmes to pull people to the museum and boost attendance figures.[3]

General films were used by 48 per cent of the museums; only 25 per cent used films on more specific subjects (e.g. a series of paintings of a particular century); 24 per cent found films useful in explaining the museum and attracting the public, sometimes using self-produced films; films were used to illustrate a guided tour (21 per cent) and—a use that continues to grow—to orient the visitor (21 per cent).

Types of audience for which intended: general audience, 50 per cent; school and university audiences, 50; training purposes, 22; to recruit members, 21; to attract donors, 10 per cent.

Museums have never gone in for film production as widely as they might, despite their wealth of prospective subjects and staff expertise, chiefly because of the cost and the necessity of securing professional aid: 27 per cent had films made for them by commercial firms; only 10 per cent used the film institutes or audio-visual departments of universities and foundations; 4 per cent had their films made by volunteers.

Museum on Film is the title of a series of five 16-mm colour films which the Detroit Institute of Arts has produced. Five years ago it began filming its art collection. It is now the only American museum photographing, producing and directing its own films about art. Films made are: *Painting in America: from Copley to Audubon*, *The Expressionist Revolt (Germany)*, two on Flemish painting and *Portrait of Holland*.

The proper distribution of documentary films suitable for museum use of films made by museums is a problem throughout the world. A survey of over 1,000 museums made in various countries by Unesco in 1963 showed that museums greatly desire facilities for showing films; that 574 museums had such facilities, but that, in half these museums, each seat was occupied less than

1. Jacques Durand, 'The Use of Cultural and Scientific Films in the Museums of the World', *Museum*, Vol. XVI, No. 22, 1963, p. 107.
2. Robert Tyler Davis, 'Publicity and Public Relations-Points of View of Museum Directors, IV', *Museum, A Quarterly Review*, Vol. IV, No. 4, 1963, p. 257.
3. Jacques Durand, op. cit., p. 106.

twenty times a year.[1] It has been proposed that an international film-distribution system be organized, sponsored perhaps by Unesco.

Apart from using their own films repeatedly for their particular purposes, 33 per cent of the museums distributed their own or other films to local social, educational or recreational groups; 5 per cent had prints of their own films sent abroad by the Department of State.

A number of museums explain why they do not use films. The San Diego Fine Arts Gallery blames limited budgets. The University of Michigan Exhibits Museum states it once had a film series but gave it up because the same audience always attended. A Science Museum in New England says it would like to use film but feels it is too expensive for the short time it would be relevant.

There appears to be a new interest in using slides with tapes. The Boston Museum of Fine Arts writes:

We have not produced many films ourselves, except as part of our television programmes; we have used slide-tapes-automated, multi-image slide presentations with sound extensively. We plan to expand both film and slide-tape production.

The Cranbrook Institute of Science in Michigan distributes films and slides to school groups for their use prior to museum visits. In Detroit, the historical society distributes film-strips free to all the local schools. The Morris Museum uses slides-tapes in place of films.

THE FUTURE

The *Belmont Report* points out that, despite the massive attendance figures (300–400 million annually), large regions of the United States are entirely without museums. Even in urban areas, it is doubtful if museums reach a majority of the population. The report agrees with the author's findings that the limited funds and lack of the special staff needed are temporarily preventing television from being more widely used by museums, but electronic video recording is expected to provide reels of film with colour and sound for use in homes and schools soon at relatively low costs. The play-back equipment can be attached to an ordinary television set. This system might allow small museums with limited space for exhibits to show a succession of exhibits from the larger museums.[2]

Finally, Allon Schoener, Director of the Visual Arts of the New York State Council on the Arts, has this to say about the role of the museum in an electronic age:

The museum's concern with communication has increased in relation to the pressure for more information from our expanding population. Because they are not equipped physically to communicate with this continuously expanding volume, the day will soon come when it will be impossible to stuff more people into museums. Communication—indirect experience—will emerge as the chief function. Museums will have to operate as electronic communications centres from which verbal and visual information will be transmitted by a variety of communication media. However, this does not mean that museums should abandon their collections of artifacts and become broadcast centres. There is no reason that museums cannot do both. In order to have something to communicate, art museums need collections. Electronic communication is a new function that museums must perform.[3]

1. ibid., p. 103, 114.
2. American Association of Museums, *America's Museums: The Belmont Report*, p. 42, Washington, D.C., 1968.
3. Allon Schoener, 'The Electronic Museum', *Popular Photography*, April 1967, p. 85.

André Szpakowski

Collaboration between museum and school

11

Collaboration between museum and school in a museum educational scheme presupposes certain conditions:

A detailed knowledge on the part of the museum of curricula, subjects and groups of subjects taught in primary, secondary or specialized schools taking part.

An educational programme, drawn up by the museum, which takes due account of the school curricula, and the collections in the museum and its particular interests.

Agreement regarding the ways in which the museum will work with the teachers in carrying out the programme in general and programmes relating to individual subjects.

Arrangements for working with young people in continuing education and out-of-school schemes.

Agreement between the museum and the schools regarding research to be done and the ways in which each side will evaluate results.

This article will confine itself to a few only of these points.

WHAT KIND OF PROGRAMME?

Although every museum—national, central specialized, general local, regional—naturally has its own kind of collections and interests, its teaching programme may often go beyond the limitations implied by its collections, the

André Szpakowski was formerly Curator of Education, National Museum, Warsaw.

period with which it deals and the territory it covers. Nevertheless, the fact that it has a particular specialization is bound to limit the type of programme it can undertake.

However rich, ambitious or active, museums will certainly never replace schools in ordinary education even if it one day happens that projects like the Mundaneum (see page 147) can be carried out.

However, despite the reservations of some teachers, museums can have a vital role in education and, in certain forms of secondary and higher education, may even be able to provide specialized training comparable to that offered by schools and universities. The number which can do so is tiny but it seems well to mention their existence, if only to recall that museums are constantly changing, have long since ceased to be mere 'cabinets of curiosities', and can now sometimes vie with universities as educational institutes in their own right.

We do not particularly want to turn museums into teaching establishments, but rather to find out what is their proper educational role, particularly in primary and secondary education. Their present possibilities should be our starting point: how can their teaching programmes effectively complement and illustrate the curricula of all kinds of schools; general, technical, economics, agricultural, training colleges, and so on.

The museum authorities, after a close examination of the school curricula, should (a) know in broad outline how these curricula are made up; and (b) draw up corresponding programmes for the museum: a general programme for the school year that includes a complementary course in any subject in which this is feasible.

The draft programme would be discussed with the educational authorities, and put into operation after both sides have agreed on it. The authorities should not simply note the programme, but actively encourage schools to follow it. Before this can happen, it may be necessary to allow teachers enough time to get used to the idea, and familiarize themselves with the details of the programme and with the museum collections. This may be difficult, but it is essential if the scheme is to work. In the past, teachers have certainly been interested in museums, but their approach has usually been passive so far as using it in their teaching is concerned.

A museum programme falls into three main parts: (a) topics which can be the subject of practical work in particular exhibitions or galleries; (b) topics which can be dealt with in museums with the help of spares or substitutes; (c) topics which it would be difficult to deal with in the museum because of the lack of display or substitute material, but which are important enough to require that the museum organize temporary demonstrations or exhibitions in its own premises, or possibly in schools.

Care should be taken to ensure that the programme does not contain gaps which would make it difficult to follow. If any are noted, either the school or the museum must do what is necessary to deal with them.

The museum programme should be built on a knowledge of what is (or should already be) known by each class or group, and what is likely to be best assimilated from thereon, with due regard to the background of students, the type of school, and the subjects likely to be of interest. For example, children living near the sea will know more about boats, fishing and the sea generally than children from Nepal, but they are likely to know less about the flora of high mountains. As the Polish educationist Okon wrote:

For anything they have to learn, children must first accumulate the experience which gives them a direct contact with the reality.

This obviously applies very much to museums, which methodically classify things and objects in order to achieve and provide a visual synthesis of phenomena and processes. A natural-history museum, for example, will avoid the accidental, the non-typical or marginal and choose specimens which are characteristic and typical, in this way illustrating specific phenomena and making them comprehensible and easy to grasp. If their resources and organization permit, museums can do a great deal for schools by providing this type of demonstration; apart from the specific knowledge they impart, they develop powers of judgement and observation in children, and hence the ability to take advantage of all exhibitions and all museums.

ROLE OF THE TEACHER

The teacher must cease to be the passive intermediary that he too often is today. He must become an organizer, and help on his side to create ways and means of collaborating with the museum.

One of the resolutions adopted at a Unesco Seminar in Brooklyn, New York, in 1952 included the following points:

Each country should set up its educational programmes and museum activities in accordance with the needs of its people.

The integration of the special educational work of museums with the curricula of educational institutions would enhance the prestige, raise the standards, and improve the methods of teaching, both in museum and educational institutions.

Teachers for all age levels should have adequate knowledge of museum resources and services. We urge that all teacher education programmes should include opportunities for training in the use of museums and museum techniques.

Commenting on them in an ICOM publication, *Museums and Teachers*, Hanna T. Rose, Curator of Education at the Brooklyn Museum wrote:

There may be those who say the teacher has no time for these extra responsibilities, no time in his training period for additional subjects. On the other hand, can a teacher neglect one of his greatest resources, especially when it is freely offered to him? How can the people of the past, be they Egyptians, Romans or our own eighteenth-century ancestors more easily be brought to life for young people than through the objects they made and used and which now are the treasures of our art museums and galleries? How can young people understand scientific developments and changes without seeing the historic pieces and models in the great technical and science museums? How can the great continents of Asia and Africa, which our western children will never see, become more than shapes on a map? Our museums of art and ethology contain the answer to some of these problems. These are the tools of his trade which lie ready for the teacher's use; these are the aids which can make his teaching easier and more meaningful. If the museums offer so much, if their values are recognized by alert educators who have experimented with their use long enough to know what results can be expected, does it not seem worthwhile to spend some time and effort to make their values available to more young people?

EDUCATION AUTHORITIES

Educationists should be fully conscious of the possibilities museums offer, and the need to take advantage of them. It must be noted with regret that the official approach is often to ignore this, or to be unenterprising to an almost unbelievable degree.

Many things accordingly need to be done: to get the largest possible number of educators interested in arranging continuous and systematic collaboration; to prepare them for this collaboration; to tell them what resources are (or are not) available; to explain the purpose and nature of exhibitions, and the scope, methods and kinds of work which can be done with the young in museums on the basis of what has been achieved at home and abroad; to keep them informed about research, and surveys regarding the attitude of young people to art; and so on.

The Polish idea of keeping the subject of the museum permanently on the agenda of regional educational conferences might be followed with profit in other countries.

The subject should also be kept well in evidence at teacher-training colleges, since so much depends on the way in which the museum has prepared the teacher, potentially its most powerful ally. And the preparation can best begin in the training college, where the prospective teacher is educated.

THE TEACHERS

A survey was made in Poland to find out what teachers think of the idea of collaborating with museums. Some understand the opportunity offered, and clearly see the deficiencies on both sides as things stand at present. But it is disturbing to find teachers, even among those doing the most progressive and interesting work, who would like the museum's educational programme to provide an exact counterpart to the school curriculum. Museums, and their workshop and laboratory facilities, will obviously collaborate in this way as far as possible. But the extent to which they can do so is limited: the museum has its own particular limitations and character. Assuming that it is rationally organized, the teacher must try to take advantage of the museum as it is; or, in certain cases, he might advise the museum on ways of bringing the content and presentation of its educational exhibitions up to date. Teachers quite simply fail to appreciate the problems and purpose of museums; and every available means should be used by the museum to remedy this position.

Five features are generally recognized as essential in teaching: (a) the conscious and active participation of the student; (b) visualization; (c) regularity of study; (d) consolidation of what has been learned; (e) intelligibility of the matter taught.

MUSEUM'S ROLE

Some educationists seem to think about the modern museum in the same way as museums were traditionally regarded in the nineteenth century, or they at least wrongly or superficially interpret the idea of a 'natural environment'. In other words, a 'natural' environment is 'natural' presentation in a 'natural' milieu, e.g. trees in orchards or in a forest, flowers in a garden, in fields or meadows, domestic animals fenced in, wild animals in forests, machines in factories; whereas a museum presents natural specimens visually in an 'artificial' environment, e.g. in the way in which specimens of plants, animals, minerals and implements are displayed in schools.

If we take this view, the museum is there simply to provide opportunities for observing particular objects, whereas it may often have a large amount of exhibition space which could be used for much wider and more constructive purposes. How indeed can anyone treat the Palace of Versailles, the Louvre, the Escorial or Williamsburg as 'artificial' environments? The apparently artificial environments of museums of archaeology, history, ethnography, natural science or technology, with their more or less ideal exhibition premises cannot be considered just as depots, unrelated to the objects they house—a picture in a picture gallery can hardly be said to be in an 'artificial' environment. But although the definition itself is artificial, it must be admitted that museum experts have as yet provided no clear or precise definition of the museum as an educational institute. Pending the formulation of something better, a museum can be said, for educational purposes, to consist of an exhibition or series of exhibitions which methodically attempt to encompass specific facts, processes and phenomena relating to art, history, ethnology, science and so on,

explaining the links between them. The educational purpose is to get people to observe, to interest themselves in demonstrations, and to make a synthesis of what they have seen.

ADAPTABILITY

In a museum programme, the methods adopted for any subject must be carefully chosen to give maximum efficiency. For example, one method will be used to introduce pupils to the everyday life of ancient Rome if very few objects that were then in current use and only a few pieces of sculpture or reproductions are available; quite different methods can be used to explain means of locomotion in the first half of the nineteenth century (for which a whole range of originals are available). The choice will also depend on the form and nature of the museum's activities, its organization, and its technical and staff resources. Methods which prove satisfactory can be definitively adopted, and used in other museums having the same teaching assignment. Here it would obviously be valuable to organize a wide exchange of experience.

To observe properly, all the senses may have to be brought to bear. The student should be able to take an object in his hands, guess its weight, see how it is made, examine its various features. This is not an absolute rule, however; handling may not be essential, except when touch is indispensable to acquiring a full knowledge of an object.

A whole range of practicals and laboratory tests can also be introduced. Let us take a practical example. In a history museum, printing should be explained not just by showing some ancient specimens. If possible, early printing presses, which can still be operated, should be available. In addition to engravings, students should be shown plates, chisels, lithographic stones and other implements, and learn to recognize them. Such terms as copper engraving, lithography, relief, should not evoke only the final product, but also the techniques used, and the workshop. This is the best way to make the most of the natural background. It is only when this stage has been passed that a visit can be made with real profit to a printing works, and the student can be introduced to the mysteries of rotary presses. If he thinks of printing only as the preparation of various proofs, perhaps in colour, from a mould, without knowing the intermediate processes, there are strong chances that his only impression will be of a factory for manufacturing papers, with a lot of noisy machines.

Similarly, students can usefully be shown how paintings are preserved; the various ways in which engravings can be made; and so on.

AESTHETIC EDUCATION

Finally, there is the question, in the relations between museum and school, of awakening the aesthetic sense and making it as sensitive as possible to beauty in general and to various forms of art, deepening the quality of artistic emotion, and cultivating a greater awareness of art. A practical introduction to the visual arts can help to develop creative powers, supplement art education and encourage talent.

Aesthetic education must fit in with the rest of education but has its own particular logic. A major error is often made by museums. A talk or series of talks on the history of art in chronological order, starting with Egypt and finishing with modern art, it is believed, will not only provide the basis for a knowledge of art but (even more important) develop a feeling for beauty and explain how to find one's way about in the arts.

Series of talks obviously have their advantages but they are merely part, and not even a very important part, of aesthetic education as a whole. They can never be a substitute for such other things as a study of colour, of light, of composition, of perspective, of the juxtaposition of colours, of the law of contrasts or for a knowledge of techniques, and so on; still less can any lecture provide a substitute for judicious observa-

tion and the real sight of an original work of art. A museum content to rely on the traditional series of talks and which does not take the trouble to try out more demanding ways of teaching is not only over-conservative, but wrong.

It is about as logical to start young people off with the study of antiquity (as if aesthetic problems in antiquity were simpler than in other periods), as to begin a foreign language by the reading and interpretation of its oldest texts. Comparisons between art and literature may be a bit dangerous, but at least we can compare the history of literature and the history of art. It is a far cry from learning the alphabet and learning to read, to discovering and appreciating Shakespeare; the way is just as long from a first initiation to the visual arts, their secrets and underlying principles, to the point where one can properly understand and fully appreciate Gericault's *The Wreck of the Medusa*. Accordingly, a course in the history of art should be introduced at the museum only when the student knows what artistic creation is about and has learned something of the ways and means in which it finds expression.

In other words, the history of the development of the language of art and of the great masterpieces should come last, and not first, in the teaching programme of an art museum.

AT WHAT AGE?

An important point arises here: at what age should regular teaching commence for children in the museum? Rather widely differing views were expressed at an international conference on the subject arranged in 1964 by the National Museum in Cracow. A majority were against intensive courses for children under 15, because their general educational background and powers of absorption are too limited. Others considered that, through fairly general courses, museums could help to enhance knowledge acquired in class; intensive courses should be reserved for the older students (16–20 years) who have acquired an adequate background in art and aesthetics. A third group which included the present author considered that every child, even if under junior secondary level, and regardless of his social background, could and should be introduced to the world of art and beauty: the only question at issue is to find how this can best be done. Is art too subtle and complex for young minds which are not yet formed or able to understand? Ways exist of establishing contact between works of art and even the youngest visitors, and some of them have been tried out with remarkable results. A phenomenon as complex as a work of art can be perceived by a child provided his powers of observation have first been suitably trained, and he has learned to distinguish certain simple but vital points and so knows also how to look at a work of art. Any institution which really wants to make art known and available to everyone should be aware of the considerable and evident differences that exist between teaching art history, and education through art—and draw the consequences.

Without surveys and comparative studies, it would be difficult to gauge how far the educational work of museums is effective; comparison would seem the only practical way of forming a valid opinion of results obtained, under different conditions, by various kinds of museums. This information would serve museums used to this type of work and others which are relative newcomers. Laying down general lines for the surveys, co-ordinating them, and publicizing the findings is something that could be undertaken by national, *ad hoc* co-ordinating committees, set up by the museums concerned.

A RECALL

Resolutions adopted at seminars tend to get forgotten as time passes. It may also be difficult to find a collection of them in any one place. Hence the following extracts from reports of meetings which discussed museums and education.

Unesco seminar, Brooklyn, New York, 1952

As museums establish respect for and understanding of the past and offer encouragement to creative progress in the future, we recommend that they should be organized so as to be available to all.

The chief aim of all museum activity must be individual understanding. It is essential that the closest co-operation be established between museums and the communities in which they are set.

Each country should set up its educational programmes and museum activities in accordance with the needs of its people.

We must realize that in the fields of pure science and applied science, which are not concerned with sensations or aesthetic values, but with factual knowledge, all spectators and listeners are like children, with the exception of a small minority of specialists. Therefore, each museum must consider carefully: (a) what can be shown in its museum that is most profitable to the visitors; (b) what can be learned as well, or perhaps even better, in publications or from lectures.

The methods and techniques of museums are well adapted for work in fundamental education.

It is essential that co-operation be established between museums and educational authorities on an international, national, State and local basis, and between both official and non-official groups.

The integration of the special educational work of museums with the curricula of educational institutions would enhance the prestige, raise the standards, and improve the methods of teaching, both in museums and educational institutions.

The attitude of museums to their material should be centred on the interpretation of their functions in everyday life today.

Museums should exhibit objects of first quality. An original object of local interest should be chosen rather than a second-rate object of national or international significance.